REAR ADMIRAL

B Y R D

AND THE

POLAR EXPEDITIONS

With an Account of
His Life and Achievements

BY

CORAM FOSTER

Including by Special Permission the Message of
Congratulations from the President
of the United States

and a Special Chapter Prepared from Data Given by
the National Geographic Society,
Washington, D. C.

A. L. BURT COMPANY

Publishers   New York

SET UP BY THE VAN REES BOOK COMPOSITION COMPANY

CONTENTS

v

CONTENTS

LIST OF ILLUSTRATIONS

ACKNOWLEDGMENTS

IN writing this narrative of the life and achievements of Admiral Byrd the author has made references to various authorities by permission and appreciative acknowledgment is thankfully placed on the record

To the executive office of the WHITE HOUSE for copy of President Hoover's message of congratulation, sent to Admiral Byrd at Little America, on his successful flight to the South Pole.

To Dr. Gilbert Grosvenor, President of the National Geographic Society, Washington, D. C., for valuable data particularly referring to the flight to the Pole and return.

To The Macmillan Company of New York for permission to quote from Sir Ernest Shackleton's absorbing narrative of Antarctic adventure, entitled "South."

To The J. B. Lippincott Company of Philadelphia for permission to quote from Sir Douglas Mawson's fine work entitled "The Home of the Blizzard."

To the *New York Sun* for valuable permission to reprint special articles.

To Robert H. Davis of the *New York Sun* for permission to quote from his interview with Commander Byrd on his return from the North Pole.

PUBLISHER'S NOTE

DUE appreciation is hereby placed on the record to the various manufacturing departments for efficiency, quality and promptness in the production of this book.

To the Van Rees Book Composition Co. of New York for the typesetting and making of the printing plates.

To the Van Rees Press of New York for the printing of the colored jackets.

To Mr. Edmund F. Chilton, President of the Standard Engraving Company of New York, for all engravings direct from originals and for the color process plates.

To the Poates Company, map line engravers, for the latest chart of the Antarctic Regions.

To Mr. Howard McLean of New York, the artist who designed and painted the colored jacket.

To the Stratford Press of New York who printed the book.

To the Grady Bookbinding Co. of New York who bound the book.

To E. Gorenflo of New York for designing and cutting the brass embossing cover stamps.

To the news photo service who supplied the photographs, Underwood & Underwood and Pacific & Atlantic Photos Co. of New York.

While all this work was done on a schedule of limited time, *all* promises were kept to the one-quarter hour designated by the superintendent of production. He recalls that not many years ago this book would be called eight thirty-two's, the press limit of those days. To-day it is *two* 128-page sheets, showing that the *Art Preservative* is still in step with the other Sciences.

The fine team-work of the men who "do things" in these organizations makes possible the production of this informative book of a quality comparable with first edition printing. *It is a first edition!*

The purchaser receives a copy of these new impressions at no higher price than the usual *Popular Burt Copyrights.* It is believed that the reading public will approve of this service to supply worthwhile and timely books, produced in large quantities, at the lowest possible cost to the purchaser.

WHEREVER GOOD BOOKS ARE SOLD

CHAPTER I

BACK in the year 1916, on one of those depressing days which commonly fall in March, a young,
alert man in the uniform of a United States naval
lieutenant, stood bleakly eying a paper which was
the death warrant for the entire plan upon which
his life had been built. The young lieutenant was
Richard Evelyn Byrd, and the death warrant was
the paper which told him that at the very beginning of his career, at the age of twenty-eight to
be exact, he had been retired for physical dis-
ability.

For many a man that would have been the end,
and pretty rightly so. Twenty-eight is no very
great age, but at the same time it is fairly well
along and when a man reaches it, and is unexpectedly blasted off the road upon which he has
decided to march all his life long, he has more
than a little excuse if he fails to get going again

with equal speed, with equal success upon another.

With Byrd the disaster must have been all the more bewildering because it had developed out of such a trivial cause. One small bone in his foot. No more than that. Failing to heal properly after having been broken years before, the bone made Byrd's foot too weak to bear him through the arduous round of his duties, through the long night watches on his ship, through inspections, through drills, through even the casual social expeditions that he undertook occasionally. Always, wherever he went, whatever he did, he limped. It was only a little limp. Most people failed to notice it at all. And a very pretty girl from Boston who had become Mrs. Byrd a little less than a year before, considered it nothing at all.

The Navy, however, felt differently about it. A limping officer? Impossible!

It is quite probable that Byrd, even in the midst of his confusion and despair, conceded the fairness of the Navy's attitude. He had always been ready to give the other fellow plenty of credit. As a youngster, playing quarterback on that football team for whose sake he had first broken that fateful bone in his foot, he always gave the other fellow credit.

12

"Not me!" he used to say when they tried to give him overdue praise, or perhaps only rightful praise, for the touchdowns. "I didn't do that. It was So-and-so. Or So-and-so. Or the team."

More than likely, as he stood contemplating that official paper which his commanding officer had just transmitted to him on instructions from the Washington headquarters of the Department of the Navy, he was ready to say, "I guess I've nobody but myself to blame."

But even though he was prepared, and able, to make such an admission he still must have been filled with an overwhelming sense of exasperation and futility. That a bone, no bigger, and probably not so big, as one of his finger bones, should have checked him headlong in the career upon which he had built his life plans. If a man had to be stopped by such a ridiculous thing, what was the use of making plans?

More than one man has come to such a despairing decision under similar circumstances. And it is more than likely that for an instant, at least, Richard Evelyn Byrd may have had the thought in mind. But there was a quality in him which made it impossible to transmute the thought into action.

13

That he did not transmute that thought into action is known to-day the world over. That, instead, he went ruggedly forward overcoming all obstacles, to hew out a new career, greater by far than any he might have had as an officer in the Navy, is now equally known. And for this the world has paid him, is still paying him, and will continue to pay him, a generous portion of well-merited praise.

Not all of that praise should go to Byrd, alone. He would be the first to insist on this if put to the question. A man is, in a fashion of speaking, what his ancestors before him were; and Byrd would be the first to say that save for his ancestors, save for the strong, resolute, adventuring men, and the brave, gracious women whose blood runs potently in his veins, he never would have been able to do the things he has done; probably not a tithe of them.

Byrd can trace his ancestors far, and as far back as he goes he is able to find some quality, some source of strength, which helps to explain himself and his achievements. Some people— not Byrd himself, nor any of his family—say that one Le Brid, who stormed through Saxon England in the van of the Norman army of William the Conqueror, was an ancestor of the Byrd who went, in storm and stress, through an even stranger, wilder land. This may be true. It may not. But whether it is or whether it isn't, there is no denying the straight unbroken line of equally strong men who were Byrd's forefathers in America.

There have been Byrds in America for almost three hundred and fifty years. As far back as 1690, there was a settled, pioneer resident on an estate which flanked the James River in Virginia. In that year that Byrd, the first of the American line, was so much a settled resident that he could send a son to the Old World, a fine suit of clothes on his back, a sword at his youthful flank, a servant at his nimble heels, a bag of gold in his not too tightly fastened pocket, to seek an education. That earliest American Byrd, no less than the ones who followed him, were stout believers in the value of books,

CHAPTER II

THE name of that first American Byrd was William, Colonel William Byrd. He left England for the good and sufficient reason that the Island was not large enough for him and Oliver Cromwell, whose democratic and determined Roundheads had taken to beheading such Cavaliers as Colonel William Byrd. Fortunately for the Colonel, an uncle had earlier gone to Virginia, had acquired ships, acres, and other property, and later had died. And it was to these possessions, just inherited, that Colonel William Byrd voyaged when Oliver Cromwell made England an unpleasant place to live in for those who did not agree with him.

The Colonel took with him a wife, of the delightful, brave sort that all the Byrds seemed pleasantly fated to marry. She was Mary, the daughter of Colonel Warham Horsmanden of Kent. The blood of kings ran in her veins and

16

MOTHER OF COMMANDER BYRD GREETING HIM ON HIS RETURN FROM
THE NORTH POLE

© *Underwood and Underwood*

Left to-right: LT. G. O. NOVILLE, GOV. FULLER, C. CHAMBERLIN, BERT ACOSTA, COMMANDER BYRD, LT. MAITLAND, LT. HEGENBERGER AND LT. BERNT BALCHEN. *Seated:* MRS. CHAMBERLIN, MRS. BYRD AND MRS. HEGENBERGER

no doubt strengthened her to remain gracious under the rigors of the hard life into which she was thrust.

It was, indeed, a life vastly different from that which she had led in England. It centred in a small stone house which the deceased uncle of her husband had built. There she lived, there she bore her children while her husband traveled afar, trading in slaves from Africa, in rum, in sugar, in molasses, sending these and other wares through leagues of wilderness to Indian tribes, to settlers on far-flung frontiers, to all men who were in a mood to buy.

This is not to say that she was left alone by her husband all the time, nor even more than was utterly necessary. The Byrds, from the very beginning, accepted that law of Southern chivalry that a man must take tender care of his womenkind. And the first William Byrd did this. He enlarged his estate, so that his son, and the two daughters who came after, might inherit enough property to keep their mother from worrying about their future. And as soon as he was able to get around to it he began the erection of another, a larger home in Westover.

It was not always easy to carry his projects out

17

according to plan. The first American Byrd undoubtedly struggled as valiantly against New World odds as his wife. No bone gave way in his foot to trip him headlong. But in a day when insurance was unknown, when every man bore his own risk willy-nilly, fire twice destroyed the Westover house. And although the first building was begun before the nineties of the eighteenth century were well along, the permanent residence was not completed until the year 1735. And then by the son, for the first Colonel William had passed on to his fathers.

Doubtless this was a pity. The third house was one which his labors should have earned him the right to see, at least once. Certainly he would have been full of admiration. For the new house was, for its time, no less than splendid—a great, stately place with wide rooms opening off a spacious hallway, with vast cellars, with imported mahogany fixtures, rich panelings, and draperies, a great mirror chastely framed in white, Italian marble, and with even a secret passageway and a hidden room or two. Enclosing the whole was a strong brick wall.

This is the house that still stands, though it has been in the hands of strangers since the War of the Revolution. The fact that it has been so long in other hands, is evidence that the Byrds had need of that resolution which has all through the years been the family's outstanding quality. That luck which dropped a Virginian estate into the lap of the first American Byrd when his English lands went to Cromwell's men, has not always followed the family. More than once, as their present-day descendant found necessary, they have had to weather disastrous storms. The War of the Revolution was such a tempest. It scattered them, as the Civil War was to do later.

It must be conceded, however, that for many years after the first William came to America the lot of the family was wholly pleasant. His son, William Byrd II, The Black Swan of Virginia, was able to provide for a private army of half a thousand men, which he kept in readiness against the Indians who resented his possession of rich acres in the heart of their hunting grounds. He could have paid these men out of his own pocket without any subsidy; but his King made it easier for him by granting, in return for his service, a tract of additional land, five miles long on either shore of the James, a mile back from the river's edge on the south side, two miles back on the north.

Of all the Colonial Byrds, this second William is the best known. In addition to his far-reaching ventures in America, he pursued a gay life in England. Whenever he went there he was, if all the evidence is to be believed, a welcome visitor at the pleasure-loving court ruled by George II. And when, not many years after the turn of the century, his father died he was able to establish in the New World one of the great fortunes of his time.

From his father, this second William Byrd inherited close to 30,000 acres of the best land in Virginia. For some years he watched this fortune pretty closely. But he was never able to stay long away from the distractions of London and it was there, in 1716, that his wife died. For ten years thereafter he never quit England. With his daughter, Evelyn, he haunted the court of St. James where she was the reigning belle. Not until his second marriage, eight years after his first wife's death, did he return to America.

When he did return, however, he settled down for the rest of his days, and until his death in 1744 he was unquestionably one of the most conspicuous figures of his period. He was made President of the Virginia Council; he was three times named Public Agent for The Court of Great Britain, and for years he was Receiver General of his Majesty's revenues. Politically he was no less dominant, and socially and intellectually he was supreme. It was said of him that no scholar wrote better English than William Byrd, and his journal, "The Westover Manuscript" offers sound proof of this. He kept a shrewd eye on his estates, and innovations in agriculture found a ready welcome with him. He was, of course, in addition, a superlative huntsman as would be expected.

On the aging marble which marks his resting place at Westover, it is written in moss-grown sentences that he was born to one of the most ample fortunes in his country, that "he made happy proficiency in politics and various learnings" and had "knowledge, wit, virtue, birth and particularly contracted a most intimate and bosom friendship with the learned and illustrious Charles Boyle, Earl of Orriery."

This on one side of a tall, stately stone. On the other side the deep carving of a patient mason sets forth that he was called to the bar of the

Middle Temple, visited the court of France and was a member of the Royal Society. The epitaph emphasizes: "Eminently fitted for the service and ornament of his country." And a historian adds: "He left behind him not only the reputation of a good citizen, but that of the great Virginia wit and author of the century."

If this last is a trifle exaggerated, it cannot be denied that he knew how to draw graphic word pictures of what passed before his eyes, and that his eyes were sharp, discerning and far-seeing. On one occasion he set down a complete, for all that it was a thumbnail, likeness of the struggling families he encountered when he traveled with the first surveyors in the great back country of Virginia.

"For want of men of holy orders," he wrote, "both the members of the council and justices of the peace are empowered by the laws of that country to marry all those who will not take one another's word; but for the ceremony of christening their children, they trust that to chance. If a parson come in their way, they will crave a cast of his office, as they call it, else they are content their offspring should remain arrant pagans as themselves. They count it among their greatest advantages that they are not dominated by the church. One thing may be said of the inhabitants of that province, that they are not troubled with any religious fumes, and have the least superstition of any people living. They do not know Sunday from any other day, any more than Robinson Crusoe did, which would give them a great advantage were they given to the industrious. But they kept so many Sabbaths every week, that their disregard of the seventh day has no manner of cruelty in it, either to servants or cattle."

His comments were not always as tolerant as these. In another place, describing some of the early residents of North Carolina, he wrote: "They make their wives rise out of their beds early in the morning, at the same time that they lye and snore, till the sun has run a third of his course, and disposed of all the unwholesome damps. Then, after stretching and yawning for half an hour they light their pipes and, under the protection of a cloud of smoke venture out into the open air. If it happens to be ever so little cold, they quickly return shivering into the chimney corner. When the weather is mild they stand leaning with both their arms upon the cornfield fence and gravely consider whether they had best go and take a small heat at the hough; but generally find reasons to put it off until another time."

A sharp, and betimes a caustic observer, this second William Byrd. But not so much the observer that he neglected his own affairs. This last is evidenced by the fact that when he died his nearly thirty thousand acres inherited from his father had grown to the wellnigh kingly proportions of 180,000 acres.

This was, under the circumstances, fortunate. The third American Byrd was a man who needed a kingly estate. His mind was full of plans and dreams royal in their magnificence even though they may have lacked the practical possibilities of his father's activities. It was he who laid out Richmond, setting it, magnificently, like Imperial Rome, upon seven hills, bringing in settlers, founding churches and schools, and keeping only a few lots for his children out of the many that he sold for a song. He sold cheaply because he liked, did this third American Byrd, to make magnificent gestures. The magnificence of his gestures is acknowledged even now by present day Richmond which has put his name on its city seal, and named a park after him.

Possibly his immediate descendants may have felt a little less admiration, for it was he who brought something like ruin to the house of Byrd. He was, to tell the truth, the worst kind of a business man. Money meant nothing to him. It was not enough that he had his splendid home at Westover. He rented another in Richmond, called Belvidere, and lived there part of the time on a most lavish scale. He thought he had so much money that he would never come to the bottom of his bags. But when he did find they had a bottom, he was in no especial wise concerned. Magnificently, he planned a lottery to rehabilitate his fallen fortunes. And it was, of course, a grand lottery. He set about to sell ten thousand tickets of which almost nine hundred were to draw prizes. Such a scheme, he felt, was sure to gain him an enormous amount of money. It did, too. It got him a full quarter of a million, a tremendous fortune for his time. But there was a catch in it. In order to make good on his prizes he offered up those lands which his father, and his father's father had gained. He offered almost all of them. He had enough ready money to go again into the most lavish sort of living. But he found himself virtually landless in a day and in a country which counted land as the only proper wealth for a gentleman.

It was, at bottom, a thoroughly arresting situation, notwithstanding the immediate and pleasant diversion of that quarter of a million dollars; and it is probable that even so gallantly heedless a fellow as that third of the American ancestors of the present day Byrd might have paused had he not been distracted by a condition which must have seemed far more ominous to the royalist that he was to the very core of his being.

This condition was the rumbling discontent heard throughout the land against that King who had generously awarded those acres on the banks of the James, "A mile back on the south shore, two miles back on the north." For by now the War of the Revolution was at hand. The century which the first William Byrd had seen in its infancy and the second had seen in its early prime was now hoary and seventy-odd. And everywhere men were talking nothing less than rebellion.

CHAPTER III

To William Byrd III, whose son, another William, had died for England on a battlefield in France, and whose second son, Thomas Taylor, was a captain in the King's army, such talk was more disturbing than any loss of lands, however wide and rich. Nor was it any the less disturbing because even such solid, consequential men as Colonel George Washington were inclined to believe that it was proper talk. The third American Byrd knew and admired Washington, had commanded a regiment alongside Washington's regiment in the army of Braddock, when that stubborn general went out to fight the Indians. But it was one thing to know and admire. It was another to agree. And agree with Washington's views Colonel William Byrd III could not.

It was an intolerable situation from the very beginning. It became more intolerable as the years passed, as war became not a threat but a bitter, unbearable actuality. And in the year 1777, on the first day of January when all the rest of his countrymen were welcoming a new twelve months, a sure harbinger of better times, the aging old royalist took his own life. In every line, however rugged, there are nearly always such weaklings. It is proof of the true quality of the line that it continues in spite of them.

Continue the Byrds did.

They were, in their immediate numbers, nine. Eight children and the widow. And this, perhaps, is a proper moment to say a word of that widow and at least several of the others of those Byrd women, gracious and brave, who came after the intrepid and delightful Mary Horsmanden of Kent.

First brief mention must be made of Lucy, beloved wife of the second William Byrd. She did little, unless it be much to have made her husband so happy that he remained eight years inconsolable in a time when swift second marriages were the fashion. But two contributions she did make to the Byrd tradition. The first was a name. One of her relatives was George Evelyn of Surrey. She must have been fond of him for one of her daughters took his surname

28

for a given name, and by one of those oddities so often encountered in genealogical records, it continued to be a favorite in the family, though among the men. There have been no less than four of the Byrd men, including the present subject of this narrative, who have borne the name of "Evelyn."

The second contribution of Lucy Byrd was the daughter, whose name has been so often repeated in the family. Around that daughter centres one of those tragic stories which never fail to stir the human heart.

It was Evelyn who became the reigning belle of London when her father, the second William Byrd, decided to remain in that city after his wife died. She was born in 1708 at Westover, and though other children came to him she was always first in his affections. Notwithstanding this preeminence, however, her life was as bitterly unhappy in its end as any young girl's life could possibly be.

There are various versions of the love story which brought about that end. The most likely is that which is tied to Charles Mordaunt, grandson and heir of the Earl of Peterborough. Young Mordaunt, unless the records lie, was distinguished, manly, handsome. Evelyn Byrd was noble, wealthy, beautiful. There was none other so beautiful in all England and if the wits of the day are to be believed, in all the Continent as well. The two seemed meant for each other. All society, all the court of St. James believed this. Save one.

Unhappily that one was William Byrd II. Notwithstanding that William Byrd II, and the Earl of Peterborough had been staunch friends something had come between them about the time that London expected to hear the announcement of the forthcoming nuptials of Byrd's lovely daughter and Peterborough's handsome grandson. It may have been cards; though this is doubtful, for both men were far too rich to find the risk of cheating worth while, even had they the inclination. Possibly it may have been religion. Byrd was not a Catholic. Young Mordaunt was.

In any event, Evelyn's father flatly, bluntly, cruelly from the viewpoint of the young couple, refused to give his approval. In a later day it would have mattered little. But in that time daughters obeyed their parents, however unreasonable their commands. They also went into declines in the very act of obedience. This is what

30

Evelyn Byrd did. She died, and it is probably no exaggeration to say that she died, as much as any one ever did, of a broken heart, just a year short of thirty.

Of her one of William Byrd's biographers has written: "Her hand was kissed by Lords Oxford and Chesterfield." Of her, "Sneering Harvey approved." She "supped with Alexander Pope at his Twickenham villa while yet the town was ringing with the success of his Odyssey; she was noticed by Beau Nash, the autocrat of Bath; saw Cibber and Mrs. Oldfield play; read Gulliver's travels as they were first presented to the public by his Reverence, the Dean of St. Patrick's, then resident of Dublin; and from the presence of an Unroyal Royalty, through a society reeking with wine and musk and snuff and scandal, passed back to her plantation home in the new country as unblemished as she came."

So much for the lovely Evelyn Byrd, unhappy daughter of the second William. The story of the widow of the third William is of a different sort. She was a second wife and from some ancestor she had received that inner strength which her husband lacked. She stayed on in the great house at Westover, harried by Benedict Arnold's army twice, stormed once by Cornwall's men. Always soldiers of one side or another were quartered in the stately rooms which once had been the pride of her extravagant, reckless husband. But she held to it until she died and her children were able to sell it and so obtain at least a small inheritance to divide among themselves. It may be that it was in no small degree due to this inheritance that several of her male grandchildren were able to climb back at least part way up to that social eminence which had been their grandfather's. One of these, a Francis Byrd, became a Lieutenant-Colonel in the War of 1812, gained distinction therein, and still greater distinction at Tripoli. In his later years he wore a sword which his State gave him for bravery in the presence of his country's enemies. Another, John, also became an officer in the War of 1812. He was killed in action.

CHAPTER IV

THE BYRDS AT THE TIME OF THE CIVIL WAR

THE third was an earlier Richard Evelyn. The records are chary of mention of him; but he must have been a rover, for about the time the Civil War started he was as far from home as Texas. In that war he served as a colonel and a staff officer of the Confederate General Corse. But more to the point, he had a son, William Byrd IV.

William Byrd IV was also a colonel in the Confederate Army during the Civil War. He and his father fought for their cause with all the ruggedness which was characteristic of their breed, and all the more ruggedly, no doubt, because they knew that for a time the Northern leader, McClellan, was pitching his tents about their ancestral home at Westover. He and his father fought, and when the war was irretreviably lost he set out no less ruggedly to salvage what he could.

In the late sixties, William Byrd IV came, with what possessions he had, up from Texas and settled with his family in Winchester, Virginia. His was the task of rebuilding in that very State in which his ancestor had torn down. That he would rebuild was likely from the very beginning, for he was made of sterner stuff than the other William Byrd who had tossed his patrimony into a lottery; moreover, he had at his side such a helpmate as the Byrds, with good fortune on their side, usually had. But there was an additional insurance. This was given by the presence in the family of a mother, who was fit to set up alongside Mary Horsmansden and that Lucy who had held to her home in defiance of both Redcoats and Colonials.

If Richard Evelyn Byrd of this present generation owes a considerable debt to his ancestors, and there is no doubt that he does, a most considerable part of that debt is due to that one of his ancestors who bore the name of Mrs. William Byrd of Baltimore. Her wealth of character was for her grandson such an example as few boys are fortunate enough to have.

As an infant, Mrs. William Byrd, born Jane Rivers, lived on a plantation in Tennessee, along the alligator infested reaches of the Mississippi. A child of seven, she traveled nearly a thousand miles in a covered wagon. The caravan of which she was a member was no place for a fearful child, and there is no evidence that she ever gave any of her elders cause to think her timid. She was equally intrepid as a Texas schoolgirl, riding her pony three miles to a schoolhouse, and later on as a young woman living in a community never quite out from under the threat of the encircling Indian tribe of Comanches.

What character she was able to demonstrate as a girl and young woman, however, was far less than she was called upon to prove after her marriage. As was the custom in those days, she married early, at eighteen. And hardly had she and William Byrd got back to the Virginia beloved by her husband, when their hopeful dreams were shattered by the outburst of the Civil War. The husband, and the young wife's two brothers all entered the Confederate army. Almost over night the Byrd lands, no less than all the great plantations of the South, were left to the care of a single woman.

Her affectionate grandsons still like to tell how well that solitary woman cared for the estate, in small matters as well as large. A favorite story is the one called the Blacksnake and the Eggs.

35

Part of Jane Byrd's task, as supervisor of her husband's property, was to watch over several hundred chickens, daily overseeing the gathering of eggs and broilers, most of which were distributed among the soldiers at the front.

One day she came upon an enormous blacksnake just after it had swallowed a baker's dozen of prized guinea eggs which had been set aside for a setting hen. Without any hesitation whatever she clubbed the snake to death, cut it open, salvaged the still unbroken eggs, and promptly put them beneath the waiting hen. That the eggs never hatched was no fault of hers.

Incidents such as this, sober enough in themselves, were the lighter side of the times. The other side of the picture was depressingly black. Reverses to the Confederate arms in no very great while were matters of common, daily report. The seriously wounded began to return home in increasing numbers and the mask of cheerfulness which they tried to wear deceived no one. Finally, for Jane Byrd alone, came word that both her brothers had fallen. And a little while after she was called upon to test her courage to the utmost. A message was brought that Colonel William Byrd also had fallen.

It may have been exalted courage, it may have been faith. In any event there was, in Jane Byrd, a stubborn something which refused to credit this last story. Steadfastly she clung to the belief that it was false. Peace was declared. No word came from her husband, but she continued to insist that he was alive. In the end she received her reward. One soft evening a rider halted outside her door, a man clambered to the ground, and a quick, debonair voice that Jane Byrd could have recognized on the other side of Jordan called out:

"Does the widow Byrd still live here?"

If the present Richard Evelyn Byrd is a trifle devil-may-care at times, he comes by the quality honestly. He had a grandfather who was no less than devil-may-care. One can imagine him planning that impudent greeting to mask his emotion while he lay, wounded and a prisoner, at New Orleans in the dying months of the great conflict.

What Jane Byrd answered is not recorded, but of a lady who could challenge a blacksnake one can be fairly sure that, after the first instant of breathless joy, her answer would be in gay keeping with her long-absent man's hail.

From the very beginning of her association with them, Jane Byrd exerted a tremendous influence upon her grandson, Richard, and his two brothers, Tom and Harry. Over the growth of these children as of her own first son she watched with the mother instinct that in her was as pronounced as her fearlessness. She guided their development, warned them of pitfalls, and followed with keen interest the progress of their several careers.

The three, she declared before the youngest was more than started in school, were in temperament as far apart as the poles over which, eventually, one of the three flew triumphantly around both the North and South Poles. As youngsters romping about the Byrd home and racing their ponies over the vast estate opened to them by their mother's kin, Harry was ever the studious one, Tom the introspective, and "Little Dick," so called in contradistinction to "Big Dick" his father, the venturesome.

How well all three learned the lessons their grandmother taught them is evidenced by their careers. Each has made a name for himself in his own field. Harry, at sixteen years of age, was manager of a country newspaper in his native Virginia. Since then he has acquired several other newspapers. He has led in the promotion of his State's welfare, and has been its youngest governor. In this last capacity he is generally conceded to have done more for the Old Dominion than any other executive since Patrick Henry. Only recently he retired, still a power although relinquishing his official status as leader. Tom won an enviable record in the World War which left him a captain and he since has become one of the ablest and best known lawyers in his State. And "Little Dick." . . .

CHAPTER V

RICHARD EVELYN BYRD, the fourth of that name in his colorful family, was born on October 25, 1888, in the quiet country town of Winchester, Virginia, the son of the older Richard Evelyn of Civil War fame, and of Eleanor Bolling Flood Byrd. He was hardly more than knee-high to the traditional grasshopper when he began to exhibit that robust adventuresomeness which so aroused the admiration of his intrepid grandmother.

"That boy is a case," she remarked one tumultuous afternoon of her grandson, still too young to start his schooling, "some day I hope, he'll write a book. He's having so much fun, and he's going to have so much more that it would be a shame to keep it all to himself." Prophetic words!

Admiral Byrd immediately on his return to New York and Washington, from the successful Antarctic expedition, will seek seclusion and write

a book, assembling his valuable and scientific notes
for an eager world of readers. It has already
been announced for publication by G. P. Putnam's
Sons, New York.

Winchester was undeniably a place in which
to have fun. It had wide, dusty streets that invited the scuffing toes of a boy of any age. It
had wide, inviting yards about all the houses in
which Little Dick became a roving visitor. And
every spring a boy could lie on his back in deep,
lush meadows and almost literally bathe in the
rich fragrance that floated over the town from
miles and miles and miles of encircling apple or-
chards in soft blossom.

It was more, however, than merely a town to
have fun in; it was such a town as could not fail
to inspire the alert, far-ranging mind of such a
youngster as the son of the Civil War Richard.
For it was the stamping ground of heroes almost
without number, and of wide variety. In Winchester, Washington had been, and through it he
had marched bent upon doing his grave, saga-
cious best to save the British General Braddock
from the Indians and his own Redcoated ignorance of New World warfare. In Winchester,
also, was the tomb of Lord Fairfax, that Colonial

41

leader, whose career set him so far above ordinary men that a boy could not help but admire, and wish to emulate. Davy Crockett was also a figure in the town's folk-lore, with his unerring rifle and a knowledge of redskin wiles, rightly the envy of every growing mind. So were Henry Clay and Daniel Webster, if a boy happened to incline toward the adventures of statesmanship. And last, but not least, were the town's stories of Stonewall Jackson, for Winchester had seen no end of fighting during the Civil War. Over the famous Valley Pike, which runs north and south from its quiet streets, the Southern General, who had been Lee's right arm, had more than once driven his dauntless gray columns.

It is not too much to say that all these chieftains of bygone days had some part in bending that young twig, Richard Evelyn Byrd IV. He could not have walked the streets their questing feet had trod; he could not have heard the tales of them that were his, for the listening, at almost any street corner, without being influenced in some degree. Oddly enough, however, the adventurers upon the sea, rather than upon the land, drew his young thoughts chiefly. Drake, Magellan, and such world navigators. Peary of North Pole fame!

There are impulses in all of us that cannot be explained, and no one can say what turned young Byrd's mind to the seas and the strange, bitter cold regions to the north and south of them. There is an apocryphal tale that his great-great-grandmother prophesied Polar explorations by one of her descendants. The prediction had been handed down as such for generations. And perhaps it was true. But something more than a prophecy must be found to explain the inward pressure which drove the boy down a straight sure road to water and discoveries. More likely it was those ancestors again, transmitting to their slim, resolute descendant the same appetites, the same desires which had driven them, too, down to the sea in ships.

Whatever their origin, the appetites and desires were there, and not to be gainsaid either by a limping foot or by other weaknesses. There were other weaknesses. Even now Richard Byrd is not a startlingly robust man; not, at all, such a burly, crushing sort of man as one expects to find in the captain of a Polar expedition. He would be, for example, a stripling alongside

43

Ernest Shackleton. And in youth his physique was still less impressive. He came, indeed, little short of an appearance that would have justified that adjective hated by all boyhood, "girlish." And he was undeniably not strong. Moreover, curiously enough he hated cold weather. His constitution was especially susceptible to the rigors of winter, as might be expected of one whose ancestors had resided in warm Virginia since the seventeenth century.

"I toughened myself by going through the winters at home with light underwear and by going without the protection of my overcoat," one early friend quotes him. "And," he concludes triumphantly, "the result I had hoped for came, for as time passed I became inured to extremes of cold."

That the ambition which could drive him to such lengths stirred early is evidenced by another story. It was quickening him before he reached the age of twelve, for in that year his diary offers stout proof of its presence. When he was twelve, in that book which grew under the steadily flowing lines that recorded his daily thoughts, he wrote that he would be the first man to reach the Pole. He was not able to make this promise good. Peary got to the North Pole while his boyish challenger was still in school. But Byrd did the next best thing. He made a similar expedition, and made it on such a scale as man had never before attempted.

And just as he set about to fit himself early to extreme cold, so he accustomed himself to the sea, and at an equally early age. When he was short of fourteen he went around the world, fighting Filipinos in the war, daring cholera and fighting in the military expeditions which followed Aguinaldo's insurrection. And his expedition is all the more remarkable because a trip around the world in the days just following the Spanish American War was a task more than one man would have shied away from, to say nothing of a boy. There were no de luxe steamers to make it in; nothing but a far from luxurious army transport and a still less commodious British tramp.

In the beginning the adventure grew out of a friendship which young Richard Byrd had struck up with one Captain Adam C. Carson, affectionately known to his intimates as Kit, who became the boy's boon companion after joining the Win-

45

chester law office of the elder Byrd. Carson's bubbling spirit and Irish wit won the youngster while Carson was drawn by the youngster's sometimes bewildering search for new things.

CHAPTER VI

THE FUTURE ADMIRAL'S ADVENTURES IN THE PHILIPPINES

SHORTLY after the Spanish American War, Carson, a veteran of that brief, costly conflict, went to the Philippines, there to become a Circuit Court judge. He wrote back to Winchester often and in no very great time came a letter containing a more than casual suggestion that his friend Dick come out and see an island empire in the making. Dick thought it a remarkably sensible plan.

"I could hardly believe my ears," his mother wrote of the incident years later (in the *Herald Tribune* of July 2, 1927). "But I soon learned that the boy was for accepting the invitation in all seriousness. He even hinted that he would run away if he wasn't given permission. I was aghast at the thought of his traveling such a great distance alone, especially since Dick was not what you might call a husky boy. But as his father and I realized how much it meant to him, and perhaps feared that he might enforce his threat to go without permission, he was told that he would be given leave.

"I secretly hoped that his desire would prove merely a boyhood fancy. I might have known better. Young as he was he had never gone back on any decision he had ever made and the day of his departure found him just as keen about the trip as he had been on the day he asked us to let him go.

"One of the most trying ordeals I ever have had to experience was to say good-by to my young son on the eve of this long journey, and in spite of myself my eyes filled with tears. His eyes were pretty close to tears, too, as he braved a forced smile and climbed aboard the train for San Francisco, where he was to find his army transport waiting."

Near to tears he may have been at the start, but no boy of his kidney could remain tearful long with such adventures in the offing, and by the time he reached the Pacific young Richard was writing back enthusiastic letters of the marvels he had already seen. He had another briefly shaky moment, for a different reason, as his transport bumped into the rough waters outside the Golden Gate. But that, too, was soon over, and thereafter he was no more unhappy than he was seasick, which was not at all.

Just before reaching Japan the ship ran into a typhoon. Once the vessel shot up the side of a wave and then dropped with such force that it seemed she must break in two. It was the worst typhoon the worried old sea captain had ever seen. But to young Byrd it was simply a situation which permitted him to have the time of his young life. The plunging, groaning transport so impressed his youthful fancy that in later years he was able to recapture every breathless, thrilling moment. It was, parenthetically, excellent training for the future leader of Polar expeditions.

At Nagasaki, Japan, the bulk of the passengers went ashore, thankful to find solid ground beneath their feet once again. Young Byrd had no more than a thought for such a circumstance, but he welcomed the variety and eagerly went exploring. Once he stood, divided between sympathy and laughter, watching a Japanese rickshaw man race furiously down a street belabored by a stoutly thumping umbrella in the hands of an indignant Caucasian woman passenger, who was plainly accustomed to more consideration than she was getting.

At Manila, Carson was waiting at the pier, his face bright with delight. The boy went ashore and there started upon a series of adventures which would be incredible were they not so thoroughly documented.

The islands were still in a social turmoil. The outlands were full of vengeful ladrones and massacres were by no means unusual.

"I remember well his first escapade," his mother wrote long after. "He was at Sorsogon, the guest of Governor Monreal. Captain Carson was holding court at the same place. It was the custom in the Philippines, on account of the extreme heat and swarms of pesky flies, to use punkahs most of the time. These were large palm leaf fans with strings attached by means of which a man, usually stationed out of sight, kept them swaying back and forth to create a breeze and blow the flies away.

"Dick became interested in the novel device and finally insisted upon relieving the punkah-puller. The work was light; too light; for in his reckless effort to set up sufficient wind he knocked the plaster off the ceiling, showered the judge, and broke up the court. When the indignant jurist ordered the arrest of the unseen offender, Dick fled. But the pursuing native bailiff, clad in little more than a breech cloth, was too fast, and he was captured.

"There followed a sober minute or two in the disheveled court room. Dick was truly contrite, and very much worried, too, before the grim-faced Judge Carson, so unlike his merry friend, Kit. But then, suddenly, as a fine was solemnly decreed, Dick recalled that all the money his pocket held had come from the very man who was now taking it away. That was something which demanded laughter. And Dick, regardless of consequences, had to give it."

There were other, equally exciting, infinitely more dangerous occasions. Byrd himself tells one of them.

"The constabulary," he wrote, "was always riding around investigating insurrections and massacres and I decided to join them. One day we rode to a village twenty-seven miles inland, and on the way back I had the closest call I ever want to meet.

"I started ahead of my party and found myself after a little alone in a village that had been pointed out as a dangerous place. The people invited me to stay, but I didn't dare and turned back along the trail to find the others. I had a pistol tucked in my waistband; but the trail was bordered with great trees and why I wasn't shot without ever being given a chance to return a single bullet I don't know to this day.

"Suddenly, as I was approaching a small stream, several ladrones with bolos in their hands heavy enough and sharp enough to cut through a body twice as big as mine, jumped out at me from the bush. They swept their heavy blades around and I whipped up my pony, heading for the river and completely forgetting my pistol. They followed, but after I got through the water they never had a chance to catch me. I never stopped until I found the detachment where I was soundly scolded for my rashness. I agreed with everything that was said, particularly as I had been almost fired upon by the advance guard as I raced forward at a gallop."

It was no very great while after this experience that the boy encountered another, even more dangerous, though of a less active sort. This next encounter occurred on Darim Island to which Judge Carson allowed him to go on his solemn promise that he would keep out of mischief. On Darim the boy found a sort of mischief he could not have avoided with the best of conduct.

"Cholera was prevalent there," Byrd wrote long after in telling of his escape, more extraordinary than the one he made from the ladrones: "Soon after I arrived a soldier came in with pains in his stomach. With a professional air that General Gorgas might have envied, I felt the man's pulse and declared him sick. The poor fellow died a few hours later.

"There is no doubt about my having been exposed to the disease, and cholera is highly contagious. That night I was sure I was going to die. I never expected to see the morning. I imagined I had pains in my stomach, too, and spent the night writing letters to my family, so that they might have a last word from me. To my surprise, and some little chagrin, morning found me with no cholera at all, whereupon I was quarantined on a hilltop a hundred yards from the camp with the doctor, a brother of Carson, and another man.

"All during the next days we could hear the groans of the men dying in the huts, and the effect on a boy was terrible. We lived on parrots and monkeys, entirely cut off from the world, depressed by the suffering below and unable to help. Finally the doctor smuggled me on a native boat and got me away to a port where I managed to get a ship for Manila."

An aging experience for a boy of fourteen. But one is inclined to wonder if it may not have been a valuable and necessary experience in the life of one who was later to bear the sole responsibility of men in situations potentially as perilous. Remembering what part carelessness as to sanitary precautions may have had in the toll on Darim Island, how careful Byrd must have been of his force through the long, Antarctic night out of which he came in triumph, his entire crew intact.

CHAPTER VII

AT Manila a somewhat chastened Dick managed to find a tramp steamer which took him farther on his world-encircling journey by way of Ceylon and the Red Sea to Port Said. This portion of his journey was uneventful, but it furnished another lesson whose value in later life may have been no less valuable than the experience in the cholera camp. Again it was a lesson on the virtue of careful conduct.

The second mate forgot to wind the chronometer, and the ship lost her bearings. The boy, Richard, was rather tickled than otherwise, for the mate, an Englishman, had teased him about the United States, but in the midst of his youthfully exuberant satisfaction he did not fail to mark the true point of the incident.

"What happened," he wrote later, "impressed

55

me tremendously. I don't suppose I had ever thought so much about navigation before. I knew the compass was necessary, and had seen the officers shooting the sun. But I did not know that time was a part of the calculations in determining position. With the discovery that it was, navigation became at once a mysterious and important function. I suppose my interest in it dates from that moment.

"I remember that we steered due west, as the only means of finding ourselves, until we hit Madagascar. Then we piloted up the coast to Port Said."

And doubtless, all the way along the shallow, treacherous Red Sea the lesson he had learned at luckily such little cost, must have driven deeper into the boy's being. Later he would remember it and profit. "Careful!" he must have whispered to himself flying over the North Pole. "Careful! Careful!" he must have whispered all along his trackless flight from America to France on the trial trip for his later flight over the South Pole. "Careful! Careful! Careful! Remember what a little carelessness once cost!" he must have whispered as he winged up from Little America, the South Polar base, on the last and most spectacular of his aërial dashes through uncharted space.

Doubtless, as he reshipped at Port Said for the last lap of his extraordinary round-the-world cruise, "Careful" was working its way deep into his consciousness, there to be ready when the moment of crisis came in the eventful later years of maturity. Indeed, it is by no means sure that it waited until then. For back home again, in the midst of an admiring, and more than casually thankful family, it was discovered that the much traveled son was too old for further play. There was the matter of education, long, almost too long unattended. After all, the boy was fifteen, wasn't he?

For Richard Evelyn Byrd education meant the Virginia Military Institute. That was taken as a matter of course, as it was taken by all the other sons of all the other old Virginia families. And as a necessary step in that earlier decision to be the first to the North Pole, young Byrd went into the academy willingly. Of his first days there a friend, later to become the sedate head of an Atlanta investment company, has given an attractive picture. For all his experience, so much wider than that of the average boy, for all his visions, so much more intentioned than those

57

of his companions, the fourth Richard Evelyn emerges as a decidedly normal, and in consequence decidedly likable, lad.

"We roomed together," Henry L. Graves explained, "and as Byrd was a lower classman he was my rat. He had to follow all my orders, so every morning he shined my shoes and saw that my uniform was spick and span for drill."

Occasionally, Graves's story goes on, discipline became advisable, and at such inevitable moments the boy whose word was later to be law to many men bent meekly for his spanking which was, one need have no doubt, severe enough to be felt through the stoutest pair of breeches.

"Of course," Graves explains, "everything was done good-naturedly. And every one knew I had a good rat. Byrd was a Virginian. He was just a nice American boy and no one dreamed then that time would make him the hero that he has become.

"In our first year, on May 15, according to custom, freshmen were permitted to wear uniforms for the first time. Of course the older men made them run the gauntlet, and Byrd took his drubbing as gamely as the rest."

He set his teeth, young Richard Evelyn did,

you may have no doubt, and saw it through. And fortunate for him that he did. He needed the practice in teeth setting. For ahead of him, and not so very far ahead either, now, was the occasion when he was to injure that confounded foot for the first time, and so begin his halting march up to an occasion when he would need to set his teeth for all he was worth, and find that no more than enough.

It is one of the blessings of this not too often blessed existence in which Destiny has placed mankind, that we are usually spared any foreknowledge of disaster. If young Dick Byrd had known what was in store for him toward the end of his stay at his beloved V.M.I., and later toward the end of his stay at Annapolis, and finally almost at the outset of his career as an officer in the Navy, he never could have managed the spirited enjoyment of life which now became his outstanding characteristic. But he did not know; and as a consequence his days were pleasant and eventful.

CHAPTER VIII

THE VIRGINIA MILITARY INSTITUTE is the sort
of place that virtually guarantees happiness to such
a youngster as Byrd was. It stands just within
the town of Lexington on a plateau which commands the storied Shenandoah Valley, its buildings gleaming whitely among the trees as one
catches sight of it from a distance. Separated
by only a few of Lexington's narrow, quiet
streets, is Washington and Lee University, with
the tomb of Robert E. Lee. Surrounding the
plateau, like the walls of a huge amphitheatre are
the rugged peaks of the Blue Ridge Mountains.

Dominating all the buildings—so dominating
as to awe such a new arrival as young Richard
was back in 1903—were the great barracks with
walls mellowed by age to a warm, grayish salmon.
In front of the barracks was the parade ground,
memorial scene of many a trying hour. Directly

across the way were the homes of the officers of the school, quaint, charming buildings, and because of the dignitaries that they held only less impressive than the barracks. Close by, sure to catch the eye of an imaginative boy, was a row of fine old French and English cannon cast in bronze, mementoes of the French and English wars through which the Colonies had struggled to freedom.

It was in this romantic environment that the fourth Richard Byrd lived and climbed from 1904 through 1907 toward the conspicuous maturity which was to be his. Too young to do any very notable thing he yet contrived to become distinguished among his fellows, an officer in the cadet corps, an athlete, a student whose scholastic record, even if it brought no outstanding praise, was at least acceptable to the most stern instructor. And always, that the audacity which had driven him, as a boy under fourteen, to undertake a world circling tour, drove him forward.

One wonders, indeed, what might have happened if this audacity had been less impelling, for to it and nothing else must be laid the series of misfortunes which reached their curiously fortunate culmination the day he made his epochal flight over the South Pole.

The whole extraordinary business started from no more consequential cause than young Byrd's decision to play football. Never a large man, nor a robust one, he was inferior in length and bulk to the run of his schoolmates on the team, but he refused to let that deter him. What if he did lack something of the height of his competitors? You only had to be high enough to reach an opponent's tackling level, and that was as low as the knees. What if he did lack in weight? Weight counted less than the drive you put behind what weight you have. He was thoroughly convinced of the truth of these opinions and how well he convinced others is demonstrated by the fact that in the end he made the first team.

Again one is impelled to wonder. Just how might the older Richard Byrd's career have been changed if the younger Richard had failed to make that first team, and so had not felt compelled to put forth that last, catastrophic effort one cool autumn day in his last year. For in all probability, if the last tiny shaving of pressure had not been exerted the foot, which was thereafter to set Byrd limping just as his most important races got a good start, would not have sustained its first broken bone.

"Hard luck!" one imagines Byrd mumbling as he quit the game. But he didn't even begin to know how hard the luck was. As far as he could see it meant no more than a little pain, a little inconvenience, and a sizable regret because he was prevented from doing what he had hoped to do for his team and his school. And one is pretty sure that when the foot recovered so completely as to cause no trouble when he went up to take his entrance examinations at Annapolis the whole incident was wiped out of his mind.

Richard Byrd entered the Naval Academy on May 28, 1908, when he was nineteen years and seven days old. His career, through the four years of his stay there, was to be a striking parallel of his career at the school from which he came—four, or almost four years of virtually unbroken success and then, in his last year, another disaster. The foot again, advancing yet another step toward its final, fatal weakness.

And once more there was no premonition permitted. As when he entered the Institute, the outlook was very pleasant, very promising indeed. Annapolis, built along the placid Severn, with its great buildings, its stretches of fine lawns beneath wide old trees was, indeed, if anything a trifle more pleasant than had been the school that overlooked the Shenandoah. And if the barracks, and the cannon, and the officers' quarters at the Institute had been impressive, how much more impressive were the great bronze doors and the golden dome of the chapel, shielding the remains of John Paul Jones. And how much more inspiring than any memento at the Institute was the cannon taken from the Spanish cruiser *Viscaya* at the battle of Santiago, was the Japanese bell brought back by Commodore Perry from his historic cruise to Japan in 1853-55? And as for other considerations, naming only a few, what did the Institute have to match the Lovers' Lane of Annapolis, or the boatsheds on the Severn with their fleet, airy shells that seemed even more beguiling than Lovers' Lane as a fellow walked past?

From his scholastic record at the Naval Academy it becomes increasingly clear that Richard Byrd was in his youth, as he is now, primarily a man of action. His record is quite acceptable. Notwithstanding that he was handicapped by a long spell of typhoid fever, he managed to pile up 622.35 points out of the 800 which were possible under the Academy's odd method of marking. And that was no bad total at all. But still, when it is discovered that the honor man of Byrd's class got the magnificent net of 759.79, it becomes apparent that 622.35 was no very great shakes.

Perhaps, however, it is not quite fair to emphasize young Dick's lack of high grades. He has learned enough since to indicate that when he sets his mind to it he can do very well. Perhaps the real explanation of that 622.35 is contained in his extra-curricular activities. Certainly these were numerous enough to explain much. Football! Track! Expert rifleman! Welterweight boxer! Wrestling champion! And in addition such gentler, but equally occupying activities as membership on the class ring committee and the hop committee. He was chairman of the hop committee in his last year, and probably a very much occupied man indeed.

He was, in addition, a very much established man. In more than athletics and the social life of his school he had gained a secure position. His comrades approved of him. Indeed, their approval on one occasion must have been little

65

short of embarrassing. For what lusty, spirited fellow of twenty-odd could fail to feel some little protest at these gentle lines, set below his picture in the school annual, *The Lucky Bag,* for 1911-12:

"Go where he may, he cannot hope to find
   The truth, the beauty, pictured in his mind."

If he did, however, he must have felt better upon reading the prose set down immediately below.

"Richard Evelyn Byrd, Jr.," this read, "athlete, leader in all right things, friend, gentleman.

"From the time we entered as plebes, until the present, Dick has been putting his whole heart into everything he does, whether it be in the gym, or on the football team, or in a little meeting that took place behind the old hospital."

Is it necessary to pause here in order to explain that "a little meeting that took place behind the old hospital" is simply a euphonious phrase indicating that on at least one occasion young Dick used his fists to settle a difference of opinion?

"No man," the *Lucky Bag* tribute goes on, "deserved more of fate and got less than he. Typhoid caught him second class cruise, forcing him to give up football the following fall. First class year—final year—injuries kept him on the side lines until his chance was gone. Then came the cruelest blow of all, just as he was whipping his gym team into shape for the season—a broken ankle."

Or, as is explained in another portion of the *Lucky Bag,* "Next Dickie Byrd tried an unheard of combination on the rings, failed to connect on the end of it and went down to the deck with two fractures and—a dislocated ankle."

In detail what had happened was this. Byrd was captain of the gym team in this, his senior year, and in order to best competitors in the intercollegiate matches he was endeavoring to master a bone breaking stunt known as "dislocating." Ominous word! This consisted of swinging upon flying rings, turning completely head over heels without altering one's grip. The arms had to be kept at full length, unbent, and the shoulders forced through with a quick jerk to convey the impression that they had been thrown out of joint. As an added attraction, young Byrd meant to make a complete turn with the legs outside, let go with his hands as his ankles passed his wrists, and catch again before he fell.

It was all a little too much. As his swift hands caught for the rings he began to fall. His fingers touched, missed, closed upon nothing and he dropped like stone, feet first. One of those feet was the frail extremity which had betrayed him at the Institute and again earlier in the fall of his last year at another football game. Weak as it was, it could not stand up under the force of his fall.

Again the fatally finicky foot. It runs, almost like a gloomy refrain, through young Byrd's years. But again, as at the school in Virginia, he has no understanding of how gloomy the refrain is.

"What next," one imagines him mumbling once more as he begins to get along, on crutches, over the wide, smooth academy lawn leading down to the winding Severn. But one doesn't for an instant imagine that he appreciated how much hard luck the accident presaged. And one feels sure that when the foot healed so completely that he was able to pass his finals and don the ensign's uniform for which he had worked so hard through the previous four years his youthfully optimistic mind held no apprehension at all.

No! That is going a little too far. From this

point on there must have been, if not apprehension, at least a shade of uneasiness. For while the foot healed well enough to permit him to win his grade, and to enter the service, it was just a little less seaworthy, so to speak, than it should have been. Throughout the next four years he was never wholly unaware of the risk he ran of having the confounded thing give way under him at a crucial moment.

That, however, is the most that can be said. The foot bothered him. That is certainly true. But it was simply another handicap to overcome, as he had overcome his lack of height, and his lack of weight, back in Virginia when he first made up his mind to play football. There is ample evidence that he did overcome it, too.

CHAPTER IX

A COMMISSIONED OFFICER IN THE U. S. NAVY

IT was in 1912 that he got his commission. And his first assignment was for sea duty. Duty at sea on an American ship of war is no detail for a man who cannot overcome handicaps. Especially is it no detail when the man is a low ranking officer. The job of ensign is not one for a man who wants a soft snap. Like the second lieutenants in the army, the ensign must say "sir" to everybody, and obey everybody, and must do most of the work aboard ship, or if not most of the work then the most wearing, unpleasant work. Especially an ensign must walk. From hold to quarter deck, from bow to stern. Up and down, forward and back.

Byrd worked, and walked. He must have limped from time to time. This is almost certain in view of what comes later. But if he did he said nothing. He went to sea, a slim, alert young figure in white ducks, and through the years 1913 and 1914 he was by no means the least conspicuous ensign in the United States service. He was a crack navigator, an excellent gunner, he was proficient in tactics and strategy. Twice he helped to put down native uprisings, fording malarial rivers with his bluejackets, fighting through jungles, and while these may have seemed insignificant to him in comparison with the tremendous affair which had just got started over in Europe, still they were affairs that gave a man experience. They were exciting, too, and in that regard at least not to be scorned. All this in the line of duty.

In addition, there were several other events not at all in the line of duty. For two of these latter a summary of the official records will do:

(a) A special letter of commendation for helping to save a man from drowning, July 16, 1914.

(b) A Congressional life-saving medal of honor for heroism in saving a man from drowning, August 15, 1914.

For a third, no summary will serve. It is not enough merely to set down that on January 20, 1915, Richard Byrd, Jr., ensign, U. S. Navy, married Marie D. Ames of Winchester, Va., and Boston. That doesn't begin to tell the story.

The truth is, to be properly told, the story would need to run to the length of a book. For these two were childhood playmates. They had been waiting to marry one another for almost as many years as they could remember.

Marriage, for Byrd, was doubly significant. It meant such a romantic climax as only few men are able to achieve, but it meant more. One is pretty safe in assuming that it meant a considerable shift in the details of the plan which the youngster Richard had announced one day when he was verging into his teens. Then, as you will remember, he had vowed to be the first man to get to the North Pole.

When very young, a year seems time enough to build an empire, and a decade seems infinity. Doubtless, when he made his declaration, Byrd saw himself triumphant at his goal long before he reached thirty. Any one of us needs only to look back upon the plans that he made in his youth to perceive the likelihood of this.

Years get shorter, however, as we grow older. Time grows fleeter with the years. A year hardly gives a mature man time to turn around; and even a decade may be too short to complete an ordinary task. Byrd was probably coming to appreciate this after three years in the Navy. And one is inclined to conclude that about the time he married he decided to take the slow, sure road to his goal.

The precise North Pole goal upon which he had set his heart was no longer possible, since Commodore Peary had got there first, a feat not to be marveled at considering that the Commodore had so many years' head start. But any program that is any good at all is susceptible of several interpretations, and if a man is determined enough he can fit one of these to his necessity.

Married and rapidly making a name for himself, one wonders just what Byrd considered his necessity back in 1915; and one suspects that it was rather less urgent than that one which drove him to his boyish vow some fifteen years earlier.

"This is a matter which can't be hurried," one imagines him murmuring. "Peary took a long time to get to his peak. And if I follow him I'll have to do something with equipment that he did not have, so I certainly can't get it over with in a hurry."

Like Maurice Hewlett's romantic hero, Prosper le Gai, Byrd was prepared by now to bide his time. And this was a shrewd decision for everything in

73

his situation urged to such an end. The Navy is no organization for a man in a hurry. Everything goes by routine in that great arm of defense. A man gets his promotions according to schedule, and all his days are smoothly ordered. But on the other hand if everything in the Navy goes by routine, still it goes and there is no stopping its course.

"It took Commodore Peary a long time," Byrd may have consoled himself, "but he got there in the end. And so will I."

Some such thought must have been in his mind when he entered the settling experience of marriage, and the slow, steady continuity of a naval career. A pleasant, successful routine seemed foreordained.

In reality, however, no pleasant routine was fore-ordained for Ensign Byrd, no matter how much the circumstances might seem to indicate one. A swift explosion, hearty enough to lift him out of his workaday road was already in the making. It had been in the making, for that matter, ever since the autumn day when his foot first gave him trouble. Three times that foot had interfered with his program. Once at school, twice at the Naval Academy. A fourth time was just around the corner. And this was to be no mere interference. Rather it was to be a complete ruination. Byrd had, it is safe to assume, planned after 1915 to stay in the Navy and take his chances. What happened a little more than a year later put a stop to such a program.

What happened was, in itself, almost as small an incident as those which had interfered with the football game in Virginia, and with the gymnasium performance on the bank of the Severn. One afternoon, at the head of a steep gangway, Byrd's ankle which all along had been giving him trouble, collapsed and tumbled him through ten fateful feet of space. He landed, as he had told himself he would while he fell, on the weak extremity. Thereafter he went into the hospital.

The Navy was as sympathetic as possible under the circumstances. He was an able junior officer in trouble, and the proper course was to do everything possible to get him out. Everything possible was done. The best surgeons of the service were called in. They examined, and consulted, they puzzled and planned.

The trouble, the chief of them said for the rest, seems to be that this particular bone is too inclined to break. But maybe we can strengthen it.

75

Suppose we nail it together with a nice, silver nail? He looked at his colleagues and they nodded approvingly.

So the silver nail was put in. And Byrd was kept in bed until, judging by all outward signs, the foot was healed. Then he was allowed to dress. And to try the foot.

It was no go. Sympathetic surgeons and senior officers, watching the young officer, now a junior lieutenant, limp gamely about his duties, all agreed it was no go. And after a time, in the routine way that the Navy has of doing important things, a recommendation was written by Byrd's regretful but duty-bound commanding officer and sent to Washington. After another time, the recommendation came back approved. The morning that it came, Byrd's commanding officer called him and broke the news as sympathetically as he could.

Sympathy, however, was of little use to Richard Byrd on that sixteenth of March, 1916. Of what use is sympathy to a man who has seen an older rival beat him to a desired goal and who, having gamely settled upon another objective, finds himself suddenly struck down just as he gets well under way?

Struck down the young ex-lieutenant must have

considered himself. It could have seemed nothing else to be retired on three-quarters pay, shelved, with a foot that was supposed to incapacitate him for any active occupation, at least in the Navy.

CHAPTER X

In the month of March, 1916, even a phlegmatic man might have rebelled against being classified as a lame duck. It was a month in which the most placid man would have felt uneasy upon a shelf. More than half the world was locked in such a struggle as civilization had never seen before, nor hardly imagined for that matter. And even an average man, though he might be by reason of his nationality exempt from the necessity of taking any part, wanted to feel that if the necessity arose he was able to share in it.

How much more strongly, then, would a man feel who all his life long had resisted the everydayness of existence, had tried in whatever way he could to make each moment more eventful, more fraught with conflict, than it seemed to wish to be.

In Europe, Great Britain and France and Belgium and their allies against Germany, Austria and their allies, were fighting battles which seemed to have no end. Their fighting was one long battle. They fought to the last ditch, then dropped into that and fought on. Especially at Verdun was this true just now. That tremendous effort of the German Crown Prince to break through to the French coast had moved into its second phase. February, and the crushing, sacrificial thrust which had gained the Germans possession of Fromezey, Abaucourt and Moranville in front of the French line of fortresses was past. General Petain, after an incredible resistance through the first fortnight of the new month, had decisively driven his enemies back off the rim of the Douaumont plateau and was holding firm. Hardly less arresting was the war in the East where Russia, still an absolute monarchy, was driving hard in the lake region south of Dvinsk in an effort to take some of the pressure off her ally to the westward. Men were sacrificing their lives in unheard-of numbers. Two million were to die in the course of the year 1917. And in America, it was coming to be more and more of a conviction that the United States would move, sooner or later, to the side of the sorely pressed French,

Belgians and British. It was the conviction particularly in the regular army of the United States and among the naval officers from whom Richard Byrd took a sober leave on March 16.

Even now-a-days there are some who insist that Byrd was always so fortunate that if he ever fell into the river he would be sure to come up with a fish in every pocket. He has been, these critics will tell you, a man who got all the breaks and never had to go against a head wind. The truth, of course, is that the determination of Byrd has made his own career. When matters were not going well he set out stubbornly to change them into something better. This was what he did after he was retired from the Navy. And even though the extraordinary result was that he finally got back upon that road of exploration which he had sought as a boy, chance, as such, can claim little credit.

If Byrd had been born lucky he would have been born with a different body, a stronger, stouter physique, more fit to stand the rigors of the career he was about to enter. The fact is that even at twenty-eight, and after years of athletic endeavor, he was still light, still slender, almost fragile if one judged only by what the eye took in. Not so very

EVA   KATHERINE   RICHARD, JR.

CHILDREN OF ADMIRAL BYRD

THE BARK *City of New York* LEAVING NEW YORK FOR NEW ZEALAND AND THE ANTARCTIC

long after Bob Davis, that shrewd observer of men who was for so long the beloved editor of *Munsey's Magazine,* said:

"Physically, he suggests a delicate instrument fabricated to the point of frailty. If one chooses to regard him as a product of evolution, it is easy to conceive that in the remote past he might have been a frigate bird winging his way across the seven seas. Even in repose he seems prepared for flight, leaning forever into the wind. In action he is Annapolis personified, erect, alert, eager. His eyes are binocular, apparently penetrating to horizons beyond human vision. From his high, Anglo-Saxon, slightly sloping forehead, the hair ripples in wave-lengths that might well have been the offspring of a steady west wind blowing fair upon him from infancy; a buoyant creature born in the breeze. He was fashioned for this generation of flyers and his pinions are poised for the air. But there are two Byrds in that body. A realist and a dreamer; a conqueror of the clouds of the earth, a commuter in the realms of the imagination."

If an observer had possessed the powers of prophecy, that description might have been applied, word for word, to the sober, depressed young

lieutenant who limped home after his conference
with his commanding officer on March 16, of the
year 1916. But, in the days immediately following, an especially shrewd observer would have
perceived that for the time being the realistic
Byrd, the dogged conqueror, was in the saddle.
The Navy had told him he was on the shelf. He
meant to show the Navy a thing or two.

For a little, doubtless because it comforted him
to work in a familiar field, he bent his restless
energies toward developing the Naval Militia of
Rhode Island. He was its commander, and within
a few months he had so improved the organization that he won an official commendation. By
1917, however, he saw that such reservist work
would not do. It was the year in which the United
States went into the World War. Even before the
actual declaration, Byrd had made his choice. It
was the inevitable choice. He laid his plans to
perfect himself in that new, almost miraculous
science and art and profession combined under
the name of aviation. In no other sphere of
activity could he have been so free of the handicap
of that frail foot; and that was enough to make
his choice certain. There was, however, almost
certainly another reason. To such an imagina-

tive, far-reaching mind as Byrd's one feels sure it was plain, even back in 1917, that aviation would be the surest road of the future to great adventure. He must have seen, even though dimly, the colossal triumphs of the years to come.

He entered the Naval flying school at Pensacola, Florida, and on the day after President Woodrow Wilson decided that America would not take orders from any foreign power, Byrd had got so far along that he was commissioned in the rank of lieutenant, senior grade, and in his old branch of the service. The Navy had thrown him out as useless, but here he was, back in, and one step farther up the ladder. He was also made assistant superintendent of the school.

The extraordinary energy which had enabled Byrd to fit himself so quickly for his new sphere is attested by the man who taught him. In 1917, Lawrence Shea, now a staid Boston business man, was a reckless pioneer in aviation, so much in the vanguard that he knew enough to be serving as an instructor pilot at the Pensacola school when Byrd arrived.

"Every moment of his time he gave up to study," Shea said some years after. "He seemed to feel that if he could only be in the air he could learn. And in order to get there he accepted invitations from any one who had a plane to use. It wasn't only with competent instructors that he flew. He would go with any one who said he could fly. He risked his life more times than any other beginner I ever saw." Twice he had crashes. Once he met another plane head-on. But he kept going.

Doubtless there were some at the Pensacola school who thought Byrd mad to take such chances. Looking back, however, it becomes fairly evident that he was not mad at all. Rather he was amazingly sane. In the very beginning of his career as a flyer, he was realizing that here he had the opportunity the Navy had denied him, and he was making the most of it. The Navy could not use a man with an undependable foot. But in an airplane a foot, good or bad, made no especial difference. That Byrd grasped this fact is indicated by the course which followed, a course which made him one of the most air-minded of men in a day when only the exceptional enthusiast was at all air-minded. When Charles A. Lindbergh was a youngster tinkering around in Minnesota with an automobile that he had made of spare parts picked up only he knew where, Byrd was an expert aviator to whom others turned for instruction.

Shortly, on top of his duty as assistant superintendent of the school at Pensacola, he was made a member of the Crash Board. This was made up of senior officers whose mission it was to study the causes of flying accidents, not so much to place blame as to recommend improvements which would prevent similar ones in the future. Even this extra work was not enough to fill all Byrd's time. Somewhere he found spare moments to study night flying, and night bombing, two subjects which had become of major importance in Europe just then and which, it seemed more and more likely, would become of equal importance in the United States. He taught these, being the first man in the country to qualify as a professor in such matters.

That Byrd was kept at such tasks, instead of being permitted to take his plane to France, will always be one of his major regrets. The foot, of course, was to blame in some small measure. But the chief reason for his detention in the United States was his extraordinary value. He knew too much to be allowed to get away. So the powers salved his protests with a promotion, making him a lieutenant commander, and asked him to substitute for battle flights in France the duties of chief of the American air forces in Canada. By the middle of 1918 he had won the official commendation of the director of the Royal Canadian Air Force and just after the end of the war in November of the same year he received a similar distinction from Admiral W. L. Grant of the British Royal Navy.

The admiral's commendation put an official period to Byrd's war days. That it did not also put an official period to his new career in the Navy proves how valuable he had grown. Discarded two years before, he now knew so much that the Navy was glad to keep him, undependable foot and all. And Byrd, once more completely confident of his future, took advantage of the Navy's attitude to urge an experiment which had been in his mind a long time.

CHAPTER XI

As far back as in 1917 the then lieutenant, senior grade, had been all for a trans-Atlantic flight by American planes. He recommended this with an all but annoying persistence, but the Washington authorities had concluded the time was not propitious. Byrd let the matter drop. He had not, however, forgotten it, and after the armistice and with peace established, he brought it up once more. In what other way, he argued, could the Navy get so much valuable information concerning flight above water?

The Navy hesitated, but finally agreed. Delighted, Byrd promptly set about testing special navigating instruments for the ships to use on the expedition. Nor was his enthusiasm dampened in the least by the Navy's decision that because he lacked foreign service he could not be one of those to make the crossing. He yielded that honor to Lieutenant Commander A. C. Read and others; and when Read, with Lieutenants Walter Hinton and E. F. Stone, Ensign H. C. Rodd and Chief Machinist's Mate F. S. Rhodes, were honored for their achievement, Byrd was well content with the commendation of the Secretary of the Navy for the work he had done in preparing Read's ship, and planning the flight.

Perhaps it would be truer to say that he was content for the time being. In the larger sense he was not content at all, as events show. They all indicate the sort of mighty, driving discontent which is ultimately at the root of all deeds of prowess; not the discontent of the envious man, but the finer, the wholly admirable discontent of one who has set himself a great example and is resolved to live up to it.

How urgent this discontent was, how relentlessly it drove him—notwithstanding such an unbroken series of obstacles as would have made the average man stop short in bewilderment, if not in surrender—is something to be considered by those, if any remain, who still insist that Byrd always had luck on his side.

For eight years Byrd struggled and got nothing but defeat for all his pains, until the very end.

His thought, of course, was to make flights, aërial expeditions of such sorts as would fit him for the great adventures he knew were awaiting men of the air and in which he was determined to have a part. On four different occasions he seemed certain of engaging in exactly the type of endeavor upon which he had set his heart. Four times he was frustrated and of no fault of his own.

In 1919, with the Navy aroused by the spectacular achievement of Read and his comrades, Byrd encountered little opposition when he sponsored an additional effort. This was a proposal to send a dirigible across the Atlantic. The C-4, an excellent craft, he pointed out, was ready and waiting. The authorities approved, told him to go ahead and, most important of all details, told him he might be one of the flight force.

It must have seemed, to onlookers, that the man who had lost his chance through a technicality when the NC fleet flew the Atlantic was to gain it now. They reckoned, however, without considering the curiously perverse fortune which never was very far from Byrd in those years. With all plans completed, with hardly any detail lacking save the final "Cast-off!" the C-5 was whipped to pieces in a sudden, terrific storm which swept the Eastern seaboard.

Whether Byrd was shaken by the misfortune is more than any save his closest intimates is able to say, even now. So far as casual onlookers were concerned, he was not. He went down, looked the wreck over, stiffened his slim, agile figure, and went about the next bit of business as though he had not lost another of the years that were becoming shorter and shorter. The next business was an attempt to persuade Congress to establish a Naval Bureau of Aëronautics. In this affair as in the dirigible flight he was a pioneer. It occupied him all through 1920, but in his spare moments, which somehow he seemed always able to find, he thought and thought again of the venture which he had all but achieved, a non-stop trans-Atlantic flight. And in 1921, on July 30, he formally petitioned the Secretary of the Navy for permission to make the attempt.

The Navy answered in the roundabout way which is characteristic of a bureaucracy. It informed him that he might go to England and help bring back the ZR-2.

The ZR-2 was a British dirigible then nearly completed. It had been purchased by the United

States Government and was purported to be the very last word in craft of its sort. It was 700 feet long, had a diameter of 84.4 feet, a cruising speed of 60 miles an hour and a lifting capacity of 83 tons. The permission to fly back over the Atlantic on such a ship must have made Byrd think that for once fortune was smiling at him. It was more than he had even dreamed of getting. He sailed immediately. In England, for days he inspected and studied the ship from which he hoped to learn so much of the subject now closer to his heart than even the stout steel ships which had been his first love. One day the ship was taken up for a trial flight.

A total wreck was the immediate consequence, and Byrd's planned trans-Atlantic crossing, on which he had built high hopes, was stopped once again. In the light of the far greater tragedy which resulted, however, he had no time for personal regrets. Flying magnificently over the city of Hull, the ZR-2 suddenly burst into flames and plunged headlong into the Humber river. Of forty-nine persons aboard, forty-four died. Of the Americans in the craft, seventeen were lost, six officers and eleven men.

"It was," says a contemporary news dispatch,

"a terrifying spectacle. About 5:30 o'clock in the afternoon the airship, flying about a thousand feet up, was first seen over the city, sailing gracefully in a softly beautiful afternoon sky. Suddenly she was seen to shake and then her nose dipped. A puff of smoke rose from her bow. This was followed by a spurt of flame. Thousands looked up, aghast. Cries were heard: 'She has cut in two!'

"This was the truth. She seemed to shiver behind a heavy afternoon haze that was like a curtain. Then six columns of smoke poured suddenly upward, and beneath these the two halves of the stricken ship, crumbling, blazing, shattered, dropped into the Humber close to the Lincolnshire shore. In the descent, men leaped from each flaming mass, spinning heavily before they disappeared into the water."

Accounts of the disaster, carefully sifted, made it plain that the huge ship, supposed to be strong enough to withstand any storm, had not been sufficiently sturdy enough to stand up under the maximum speed of which her own engines were capable.

This was a discovery which Byrd helped make. The knowledge, together with such other information as was gleaned from the wreck, was the sole fruitful result of the disaster for him. He managed to glean so much from the work of salvage and the investigations which followed. And with this he came home bearing also the commendation of the Secretary for the Air of Great Britain for his heroism in the rescue work.

The purpose which had by now become the center of his thoughts, however, was as far from culmination as ever. And two years more passed, quickly, as now they seemed always to pass. In the first of these, Byrd made such progress in his study as is indicated by the fact that he established and organized the Air Reserve for the United States. And in the second, 1923, at least he must have solidified his position, for he received another of those official commendations which, by now, had come to be hardly exciting. For all he had done in behalf of the Air Reserve, he received the formal approval of the General Staff of the United States Navy.

Then, in 1924, his hopes found cause to rise again. He was assigned to the dirigible Shenandoah, and the purpose of the assignment was to make him one of a party which was to fly the dirigible across Alaska and over the North Pole.

CHAPTER XII

IT had finally come, the seemingly sure promise
of a fulfillment of the boyish dream: not the precise fulfillment, but one even more splendid though
of a different sort. He was not going to be the
first man at the Pole. Peary had been there. But
he was going to be one of the first to reach it by
air. He would not be able to make the record he
had vowed to make; but he would make a record
on which he need look with nothing short of
hearty pride.

He began to study and plan. Once more he
lived so much with his ship that he seemed almost
a part of it. Watchmen making their rounds by
day and night were surprised not when they did
see Lieutenant Byrd, but when they did not see
him.

Once more, for the third time, all his plans

were brought to nothing. Like the C-5 and the ZR-2, the Shenandoah also met with disaster. She, also, went up on a test flight. With forty-three persons aboard she left her hangar at Lakewood, N. J., "with everything functioning normally," as the report later put it. The purpose was to make a long trial run into the west. At midnight, after an all-day voyage among the clouds, and after having escaped a severe storm, the craft suddenly, and for a reason not apparent at the time, began a swift ascent. A considerable amount of gas was valved out, whereupon she began a descent almost as rapid. Now ballast was tossed overboard, and she shot up again. More gas was valved away. She dipped, bent, then unexpectedly broke in two. One heavy half of her, emptied of its supply of gas, plunged to the earth. The other, with full, unbroken compartments, came down so slowly as to save the lives of the men in it.

Professor George L. Clark, director of the research laboratory of the Massachusetts Institute of Technology, concluded that defects in the metal work were responsible for the disaster.

"The results of our investigation," Byrd read, "do not place the responsibility for the crash upon the manufacturers of the metal. It was merely a case of inadequate research." This, and much more Byrd read, for once again he was gleaning what benefit he could out of the wreck of the ship which, had it remained whole, would have taught him so much more. Once again, he was the recipient of that oddly good-bad luck which left him whole, but brought his high hopes to nothing.

Three times, in something like five years, his plans and hopes had been frustrated. If he had not been driven by the admirable discontent which was so deeply buried in him, he would, probably, have given up. But that was so urgent a force in his life that it enabled him to survive still another disappointment.

In the same year that the Shenandoah fell, Raold Amundsen, the Norse explorer, was planning just such another flight into the North as the Shenandoah was to have taken. He needed experienced aviators to manage three supplementary planes which he proposed should accompany his dirigible, and he invited the United States Navy to supply one of these. The Navy accepted the invitation. Byrd promptly applied for permission to go. He was as promptly rejected.

Eleanor Bolling, THE SECOND SHIP OF THE BYRD ANTARCTIC EXPEDITION

© *Underwood and Underwood*

THE WHALER C. A. LARSEN LEAVING LOS ANGELES HARBOR FOR NEW ZEALAND. COMMANDER BYRD, HIS FLYING STAFF AND OTHERS OF THE EXPEDITION, ARE ABOARD

The reason? No! This time it was not the bad foot. It was his marriage. The Navy decided that a married man had too many responsibilities to make the flight.

And then, as if he had not received heavy blows enough, he was retired again. Some one in Washington, doubtless, had recalled that undependable foot. And by this time his services were apparently less valuable. Seven years had passed since he had been taken back into the service. Many men had learned to fly.

Byrd took his retirement soberly, as he had taken the one back in 1916. But then he did what men who are possessed of the greater discontent are compelled to do. Deprived now of any hope of going on a naval aërial expedition of magnitude, and notwithstanding the setbacks which he had suffered, setbacks which would have made many a man fear his own ability, he promptly set about organizing an Arctic expedition of his own, an aërial Arctic expedition, of course.

Byrd could not know it at the time, but the turning point had come. He had had his lean years. Now the fat were awaiting him. And he was ready. For almost ten years he had been preparing, studying, storing up knowledge. Now, just when he was filled to the bursting point, he found the opportunity to use all he had acquired. It wasn't given him. There was no business of pure and simple luck about it. He made his position by going out and inspiring the material assistance without which he could have done nothing.

In 1926 the old boyish dream, which was to reach the well-nigh incredible climax in 1929 above the South Pole, entered its first stage of reality. In that year Byrd made, successfully, his first Polar flight. Early in April the steamer *Chantier,* carrying the Commander and forty-seven volunteers, sailed out of New York Harbor with a blue and gold pennant flying from its masthead and farthest north as its goal. The man who was not strong enough to serve in the United States Navy was off on the first of two expeditions which were to equip him with that information which he needed to carry through the crowning achievement of his middle life—the dramatic expedition into the Antarctic, the spectacular flight over the South Pole.

Shortly before he set sail, Byrd gave public thanks to the men who had made his expedition

possible, his financial backers—Edsel Ford, John
D. Rockefeller, Jr., Vincent Astor, A. L. Froth-
ingham of Massachusetts, Dwight W. Morrow,
Thomas Fortune Ryan, Porter W. Adams, William Schiff, Godfrey L. Cabot, R. F. Hoyt, P. W.
Rouse, William A. Read, Captain and Mrs. Gib-
bons, Lorillard Spencer, the Standard Oil Company of New Jersey, Robert W. Russell and
William H. Todd.

These were the men who had supplied him with
his ship, and had filled her hold with boxes, bat-
teries, bags, barrels, crates, skiis, and a wealth of
miscellaneous stores. These were the men who,
most important of all, had supplied the giant
Fokker plane which was to be used in the final
dash to the top of the world, and the fleet Curtiss
Oriole, the auxiliary ship of the air. The rescue
ship, too, in case a rescue ship happened to be
needed.

These backers were foremost among the thousands who waved Byrd a hearty farewell as he
got his ship hastily underway. His was a hasty
departure because inevitable delays had held him
a considerable time after his planned day of leaving and it had become necessary to push on with

all possible speed in order to get in his exploration expeditions before the advent of the dense fogs which always occur late in the Arctic Spring. Such fogs conceal the earth, making flying useless and well-nigh impossible.

There was another, equally legitimate need for speed. Byrd was only one of three men leading expeditions into the Far North that year. Captain George Wilkins was at Nome, Alaska, with both dogs and planes, preparing to cover virtually the same territory that had been included in Byrd's program. And in Rome, amid the cheers of a huge crowd, Captain Raold Amundsen, commanding the Amundsen-Ellsworth Mobile expedition, was getting away for Oslo, Norway, whence he planned to start on a dirigible flight which would also overlap, in its purpose, the Byrd expedition.

With his crew of forty-six men Byrd sent the unpretentious *Chantier* rapidly down the bay and out into the ocean. Chief among his companions were:

Floyd O. Bennett, aviation pilot, United States Navy, second in command.

Lieut. G. O. Norville, U. S. N., third in command and flight engineer.

Lieut. Alton N. Parker, U. S. M. C. Reserve, pilot.

William C. Haynes, meteorologist, United States Weather Bureau.

Dr. Daniel O'Brien, physician of the expedition.

T. H. Kincaid, engine expert, Wright Aëronautical Corporation.

L. N. Peterson, mechanic.

All stout adventurers, and that they were assumed to be stout eaters, too, was attested by the provisions in the hold—400 pounds of pemmican, 4,500 pounds of whole carcass beef, great stores of corned and dried beef, mutton, pork and fowl, frozen; five hundred and forty dozen fresh eggs, huge tubs of butter and lard and cheese, and 950 pounds of bacon. This last was an innovation. Earlier explorers had decided against bacon, but Byrd wanted some of the rich, compact meat.

The chief objects of the expedition were to charter new lands, and this alone made it important that Byrd get in ahead of Amundsen who would, naturally, have claimed any new territories that he found in the name of his own country; to compile data which would be of benefit to commercial aviation; and to gather information of value to the Federal meteorological service. The dramatic climax of the whole endeavor was to be a flight, or at the worst an attempted flight, around the North Pole.

CHAPTER XIII

Up in Alaska Wilkins was supplementing his
planes with veteran sled-dogs; but Byrd proposed
to use none of these.   He took a couple of hand
sleds; but if his plane failed on its Polar flight
he and Bennett would have to drag the sleds,
loaded with scanty provisions, themselves all the
way back to their base of supplies, or to whatever
solitary habitation they were lucky enough to find
in the Arctic wastes.

"We are pinning our faith on planes," Byrd
said.   "In this way I hope to demonstrate the
practicability of heavier-than-air machines.   If
the planes can conquer the Arctic, certainly no one
will then deny that they can conquer the less
rigorous regions of the earth."

According to the general plan, the *Chantier*
touched first at Tromso, Norway, and took aboard
a skipper who was accustomed to bucking the ice-

filled Arctic sea. Then she sailed directly for Kings Bay, Spitzbergen, which was made the base of operations for the earlier stages of the expedition. From Spitzbergen, also, Byrd made the aërial journey of which he had dreamed so long, the flight over the Pole.

This was by no means the easy achievement that modern planes and improved engines would make it seem to be. A year earlier the same Amundsen and Ellsworth who were even now challenging Byrd to a race, had tried and had come down 150 miles short of their goal.

Byrd, however, was utterly confident of his ability, and the ability of his assistants, to plan and execute the flight successfully. Even as he was preparing for the attempt he predicted that in a very few years the effort he was making would seem as nothing, that by then great passenger ships of the air would be soaring over the top of the world on regular schedules.

Perhaps some of his confidence was peculiarly personal. This is likely because of the fact that the navigating instruments which he intended to use were to no small degree of his own invention. These included, besides four compasses, a bubble sextant of his own devising. This instrument was far superior to the ordinary sextant in ascertaining angular distances so as to enable the user to reckon altitudes in such a way as to ascertain latitude and longitude; in a word, to locate himself within a mile or little more.

Byrd also spoke very highly of the efficiency of the Bumstead sun compass devised in the offices of the National Geographic Society by Albert H. Bumstead, the Society's cartographer.

Byrd's plans called for an arrival at Kings Bay about May 1. He managed to do even a little better than this. By driving his ship, and by taking advantage of every opening, he made his objective on April 29. He proposed to spend some two weeks in preliminary survey work, and get off on his Polar flight about the middle of May. This program, also, he bettered. Almost, one would be willing to risk saying that after long years of making his luck, Byrd no longer needed to force it. Fortune, at last, seemed on his side. Those heavy fogs which he feared were in the making, but he got in ahead of them, and on May 10, with Floyd Bennett as co-pilot, he soared up from Kings Bay, darted away into the white wastes to the north, disappeared from sight, and was gone for just a few minutes, nine to be exact, under sixteen hours.

When the great Fokker plane droned into sight again its commander and his co-pilot had done what only two other men in the history of the world had done. They had reached the top of the world. The other two men were Commodore Peary, who had destroyed Byrd's hope of being the first man to reach the North Pole, with his faithful companion, Matt Henson. These two had achieved their victory on April 6, 1906, after having been out of contact with civilization 429 days. It is a striking commentary upon the well-nigh incredible pace of the world's progress in this twentieth century that only twenty years and a month and a few days later, Byrd was able to reach the same objective in two-thirds of a day, and come back with data of great scientific value.

How valuable Byrd's data was is evidenced by the tide of congratulations and approval and commendation which rose at once to sweep in upon the victorious commander in his rude quarters in Kings Bay. Governmental leaders and men of science, military chiefs and aviation experts all joined in this well-merited praise. President Coolidge hailed the triumph as proof of the high development of aviation in this country. Incidentally, President Coolidge, notwithstanding a considerable amount of criticism leveled at Byrd for attempting the expedition by plane, had from the first been in full accord with the program. General Pershing, ill in Washington, cabled from his sick bed: "It was a wonderful achievement. It ought to make every American stand up a little prouder to-night." Anthony Fokker, designer of the plane in which Byrd had made the flight, was especially impressed by the fact that the daring effort had indicated the practicability of airplanes in extremely cold regions. And in the office of the Federal hydrographic bureau, the Carnegie Institution, and the National Geographic Society there was equal enthusiasm, for it was felt sure Byrd had obtained data of great value to science.

Byrd came home to receive such tributes as are granted to only a few men out of every generation. He was back by June 24, again making a quick and fortunate voyage. Thousands acclaimed him wherever he went, but he said, as he had in the days when he played football: "Don't give the credit to me. It was team work that did it." There were hardly words enough to measure his achievement, in the verdict of the nation.

107

In all the length and breadth of the country there was, doubtless, only one man, Byrd himself, who was inclined to minimize the achievement, to call it, at best, no more than a trial flight. And he was, as a matter of fact, too busy to speak. He was, however, already actually considering an expedition which was to be so much vaster in magnitude as to make the North Polar flight seem little more than an afternoon outing. He was already looking as purposefully toward the bottom of the world, as once he had looked toward the top.

CHAPTER XIV

BYRD DECIDES TO TRY FOR THE NEW YORK TO
PARIS SINGLE-HOP FLIGHT

THERE was, however, to be a slight interruption
to this new project. Not an unlucky one; Byrd
seemed to have left obstacles behind somewhere.
But still an interruption of sorts. The surface
explanation was that Byrd decided to try for a
$25,000 prize offered by Mr. Raymond Orteig of
New York to the first flyer who got across the
Atlantic from New York to Paris in a single hop.
It is only fair to Byrd to suggest that he had a
more consequential motive than this. In all prob-
abilty he was still not satisfied with his knowledge
of aviation. True, he had proved a plane could
he raced 1,600 miles through the bitter cold temperatures of the Arctic regions. But wouldn't one
be able to prove other points, equally important, if
one attempted a more than 3,000 mile non-stop
flight over water? Wouldn't one, for example,
find out valuable facts about the effect of moisture

upon an engine, and about air currents, to say nothing of the tremendously important value that would come in the name of Experience?

As early as in October of 1926, less than three months after his return from Kings Bay, Byrd was hinting at the ocean flight. By February, it was definitely known that he would make the attempt. Rodman Wanamaker of New York, always an enthusiast in matters pertaining to aviation, furnished the money the explorer needed to make the venture the scientific success it was meant to be. A cool half million is the figure commonly reputed to have been provided, and Byrd went to work with a will, giving infinite attention to his whole program. What he desired was to produce the most complete scientific results possible. He drew upon every source of meteorological information, both in this country and abroad. He procured every possible scientific aid to navigation and safety. Nothing which could have contributed was overlooked.

Naturally, Byrd would have liked also to be the one to command a non-stop flight across the Atlantic. That spectacular climax to the more practical achievement would have been more than gratifying. But another man got in ahead of him.

There were, at that time, three planes being groomed for the dash, an odd parallel to the three expeditions which had set out for the Polar regions the year before. And another of the trio was to get across first, the slim, boyish adventurer who had come unannounced from the Middle West in a plane named the Spirit of St. Louis won the honor.

"I'm Charles A. Lindbergh," he exclaimed when his silver bird lighted gracefully and magnificently at Le Bourget, the flying field outside Paris. And while he was yet dazed at the tumult which swirled around his gallant head, he got Byrd's heartiest, and one can be sure, sincere congratulations.*

And thereafter, as soon as he could get his huge, three-motored machine into the air with its overwhelming load of necessary fuel, and in spite of bad weather conditions, Byrd followed.

And doubtless because he was following, because he was not disturbed by the glamorous prospect of being the first to Paris, he was able, in the course of his flight, to pay more attention to the

* For Col. Lindbergh's amazing career see the book, "Lindbergh, the Lone Eagle," by George Buchanan Fife, published by A. L. Burt Company, New York.

considerations which were, after all, his chief motive. He studied air conditions at different altitudes as his plane went swiftly above the waters. He checked wind velocities. He made careful notes on high and low pressure areas. He learned something of fog banks. He discovered means of avoiding ice formations on the wings and propellers of his plane. He watched with an unfailing eye the whole array of precious, accurate instruments which filled the face of the pilot's cockpit forward. Up to 18,000 feet, which was the ceiling for his heavily loaded, heavy ship, he checked his observations and set down his data in careful, precise, legible notes.

Probably one of his greatest achievements on the trip was to prove the value of radio in such a situation. Lindbergh's plane had no radio. Byrd's carried the most powerful that could be mounted. He was able to establish a 1,000-mile daylight range in communication with Roosevelt Field, Long Island, his point of departure, and he managed the more extraordinary distance of 1,600 miles in talking with the Radio Corporation of America at Chatham, Mass. Nothing like it had ever been achieved before.

Byrd's plane, the America, was not quite able to

make Paris, and so at least duplicate the great feat of Colonel Lindbergh. It came down in the water at the edge of the seaside village of Ver-sur-Mer, with him and his three rugged comrades, Bernt Balchen, Bert Acosta, and George Noville. It was only after this mishap that the four got their plane into the air again and finally made their goal.

A disappointment, certainly. But possibly the disappointment was lessened by the fact that Ver-sur-Mer is very close to the probable spot from which that reputed ancestor of Byrd, Le Brid, took ship with William the Conqueror for the British Isles back in the eleventh century. It cannot be such a great disappointment to a man to find himself back in the home region of his early ancestors.

Indeed, it could hardly have been any disappointment at all, that drop into the smooth sea before Ver-sur-Mer, for, after all, the fundamental purpose of the flight had been achieved.

"A splendid performance," said observers. "It will furnish data which should be of immeasurable help in future flights between America and Europe."

Byrd, receiving honors in France, and later receiving more in America, let it go at that. Poincaré, premier of France, made him an officer of the Legion of Honor. He and his comrades were given an ovation at the Paris City Hall. They were hailed as unofficial ambassadors of Good Will.

Byrd continued to say nothing. If all the world proposed to act as though there was nothing left for him to do, it was the world's own affair. But as for himself, his thoughts were already turning away from what had happened to what he meant to make happen. The flight to France, important though it had been, was simply one more stepping stone. He had gone a little higher, to another vantage point from which he could see a little more clearly.

There had been, in his almost forty years of life, a number of such stepping stones. One had been that boyish adventure, the cruise around the world. It had aroused his interest in navigation. Others had been his years at school. They had taught him leadership, and no less essential, an unyielding stubbornness in the face of setbacks. His time in the Navy had helped him up another notch. So had his lessons as a flyer, and his work as an instructor of flying. With that undepend-

114

able foot he had gone up, haltingly, but steadily from one of these to the other. Then, at the last he had got through his two long flights. Stepping stones all. Now he was up so high he could look into the distance for a new goal. Rather he could look at one. He had no need to hunt it out. He had marked it long before. Even before he had started to France he had spoken about it. If the public had forgotten in its excitement over his achievement, he remembered. And while all the world acclaimed him his eyes were turned to where the Antarctic sea rolled, to where crashing floes set up a barrier that he was sure would prove far less formidable than appeared from his present distance.

Once the trans-Atlantic flight was over and done with, Commander Byrd became so full of his new project that it would have been impossible, assuming this had been necessary, to keep the world entirely ignorant of his plans. One sees him, in the very midst of his honors in France, getting away behind locked doors with his closest companions, Bennett and Balchen, and talking up the South Pole until he had fired their enthusiasm into a flame as hot as his own.

CHAPTER XV

THE America to Ver-sur-Mer crossing was completed early in June of 1927. By the end of that month the newspapers of both Europe and the United States were full of preliminary announcements of the vastly larger project. Most of these were pretty far from the truth. It was announced that Byrd proposed to make the entire flight by air, and for a while great space was given over to speculations as to what type of plane would be used. It was announced that the expedition would start within a month, within two months, certainly not later than the coming autumn. Byrd, himself, never had shown any inclination to rush headlong into reckless ventures; but the public seemed determined to get him off on this new and greatest one with no preparations at all. And perhaps Byrd's own preoccupation with the project justified this impulsive desire. He was so intent upon it that upon his return from France he refused countless invitations to visit cities all over the country and receive additional honors.

"Too busy preparing for the Antarctic expedition," he announced, with an appreciation that was no less great because it was succinctly phrased.

Small wonder that onlookers felt that such absorption must mean a swift beginning. Some were so sure of this that they set the month, the following October, and then the day, the twentieth. But as early as in July, Byrd had emphasized that it would be impossible for him then or in the near future to fix the time. And then, for the first time, he tried to give some indication of the scope of his plans, pointing out that an expedition which resulted in no more than a flight to the South Pole would be of virtually no value. What he hoped to do, he said, was to gather information which would be of use to all scientists.

This declaration, however, failed to end the rumors. They did not stop until in August when Byrd definitely announced that the magnitude of his undertaking was such that he could not complete his preparations until the following year. At a rough guess, he announced, he would get his party, with its supplies and equipment, away from the United States some time in the autumn of 1928.

Admittedly, he was delaying long in his attempt to conquer the South Pole by air. "But when I do start," he said, "I hope it will be a success in every sense of the word."

Coincidentally with this announcement he quashed public gossip which was endeavoring to make his expedition a challenge to another South Pole exploration venture that was being promoted by the English Sir George Wilkins, who had also been in the Far North while the Byrd unit was occupied there. He pointed out that the plans and purposes of the two groups were so different that there could be no possible suggestion of rivalry; and after much effort he managed to drive this belief home by calling attention to the fact that the two forces would be operating in entirely different areas.

That bothersome and doubtless slightly embarrassing circumstance cleared away, Commander Byrd set about to formulate a program. Before he did anything else, he had to have a detailed outline of what he proposed to attempt in the Antarctic. Only with this in his possession would he be able to settle upon the length of time he would need to stay in the Far South. And only after he had decided this could he settle upon the provisions and equipment that would be necessary for a large personnel.

The preliminary announcements of his program had no more than been given out than it became apparent that the Commander was projecting an undertaking of such magnitude that it would surpass all previous Polar explorations, either North or South.

The country was thinking of little but the actual flight by airplane to the Pole and back from whatever base Byrd decided upon. His first statement made it clear that he considered that to be of comparatively little consequence.

"The Pole," he said bluntly, "is the least of our goals."

Far and away ahead of the Pole in consequence, he pointed out, were the scientific investigations which he proposed to make, and for which he was already recruiting such a corps of experts as no other similar expedition had ever had.

One of his chief hopes was to establish whether the vast Antarctic continent, measuring some 2,000,000 miles, was a single unit or was divided by water. If it was so divided he hoped to locate these straits, or some of them. Another problem, which he would endeavor to solve for scientists who had been puzzling over it for years, was whether Antarctica, still in a glacial period, ever had been inhabited by man or ever had been used as a passageway between the Old and the New Worlds by migrating peoples. He meant, moreover, to attempt to discover the relationship, if any, between the southward extending Andes Mountains of South America and the tall ranges which were known to exist on the Polar continent still farther south. For the benefit of scientists already enormously interested, he announced specifically that he proposed, if possible, to investigate:

(1) The potential gradient of the atmosphere, making a record of a year or longer with equipment furnished by the Carnegie Institute.

(2) Auroral phenomena.

(3) Earth radiation, and thermometric conditions.

(4) Sky radiation.

(5) Radio activity of snow, ice and such geological specimens as might be found.

(6) Penetrating radiation.

(7) Ionic content of the atmosphere.

(8) Conductivity of the atmosphere.

(9) Glaciology; crystallographic structure of the ice.

(10) Correlation of atmospheric humidity with atmospheric electricity.

(11) Gravimetric determinations.

(12) Oceanography and hydrography. In this connection he meant to make a Plankton collection, obtain records of marine microörganic photo-microscopy, and make tests for depth, temperature, salinity and color of ocean bottom wherever possible.

(13) Magnetic phenomena, making records through a period of a year or more of total and horizontal intensity and declination for the Carnegie Institute.

(14) Dip circle determinations of F.H. and D. from as many field stations as possible.

(15) Directivity of static.

(16) Fading of radio signals.

(17) Kenally (heavy side layer) determinations.

(18) Echo signaling and circumterrestrial measurements.

(19) Temperatures.

(20) Wind velocities.

(21) Barometric phenomena.

(22) Upper strata work.

(23) Humidity.

(24) Pathological reactions of personnel to various climactic and dietetic conditions. General records on personnel under above conditions.

In addition he proposed:

(a) Detailed mapping of the main base and its environs.

(b) Exploration and mapping of as much of the coastland of King Edward VII Land as is possible by whatever means of transportation are available.

(c) Mapping and study of mountains with reference to structure, trend, materials, with a view to determining any possible relationships to those of New Zealand.

(d) Collecting of rock specimens in situ, both for later petrographic study and for study by the geophysical laboratory at Washington, D.C.

(e) Exhaustive search for fossils, either from rocks in situ or from the glacial drift—these will indicate what the past geological history and climate of Antarctica has been.

(f) Mapping of any new routes or places visited by members of the expedition.

(g) Study of glaciers from the geological viewpoint—especially by way of comparison and contrast with those studied in Greenland.

(h) Collection of natural history specimens that can be preserved by salting, to be later studied and mounted by such museums or institutions as may be the recipients of such collections.

It was a tremendous program. Few men would have dared go so far as propose, let alone announce an intention to carry it through. But authorities in general were prompt to profess a conviction that Byrd would be able to do pretty much what he was planning. The National Geographic Society, from its headquarters in Washington, D.C., was prompt to prove its confidence by contributing $25,000 to help defray the expenses of the expedition. The Society was eager for new and detailed information from such a rich field for the collection of scientific data, and from one so little disturbed. Later the Society generously contributed a second $25,000.

What other explorers thought of the project

was pretty well indicated by a statement made about this time by Commander Douglas George Jeffrey, R.N., D.S.O. retired, an Englishman who had been navigator and magnetician with Sir Ernest Shackleton on the expedition in which the latter lost his life in 1921-22. Jeffrey gave it as his opinion that the magnitude of Byrd's expedition offered an unparalleled opportunity for investigation of the cold continent at the bottom of the world which, despite its inaccessibility and barrenness, exerts such influence upon life on this planet, even thousands of miles distant.

Byrd had, Jeffrey said, the chance to clear up many of the mysteries of the South Polar regions which had puzzled and fascinated scientists for years.

"It is known," Commander Jeffrey declared, "to both scientists and men of the sea that there is a strange, intimate connection between Antarctic weather and the height of floods of the Egyptian Nile. Meteorologists also link the monsoons of India, and even certain conditions in distant Iceland, with the Antarctic weather."

The Commander pointed out that such tidal and atmospheric influences of the South Polar regions upon the rest of the globe had been indicated years before by Lieutenant Matthew Fontaine Maury, the American naval officer, in his book, "Physical Geography of the Sea." "Maury," said Jeffrey, "declared the vast spaces about the South Pole to be 'a reservoir of dynamic force for the winds, and a regulator in the grand meteorological machinery of the earth.'

"Such theories," Jeffrey concluded, "and the many seemingly improbable influences traceable to the South Polar region, need just such intensive, prolonged study as Commander Byrd is preparing to give."

One curious circumstance, concerning which Jeffrey, the National Geographic Society, and scientists and explorers in general, were especially hopeful that Byrd would be able to explain, at least in part, was the utter absence of animal life and vegetation in the Far South. In the North Polar regions had been discovered plant growths, at least of a sort, and animals such as bears, musk ox, wolves, rabbits. In similar areas adjacent to the South Pole there were only penguins and such creatures from the sea as seals and whales. The lower temperatures were a partial explanation, but it did seem that there should be a more fundamental one and it was hoped that Byrd would bring back a clue if no more.

It should be plain, by this time, that although Byrd was taking upon himself an enormous task the world in general was putting upon him one at least as large. And this inclination to burden him was a striking reversal of the opinion which the United States Navy had felt compelled to give out so very few years before. The man the Navy had decided was unable to bear up under active duty was now being encouraged in an activity so much greater that any the Navy had ever asked of him that the contrast was ludicrous.

In justice to the Navy, however, it must be admitted that Byrd had had, and for that matter still had, the undependable foot. It must be admitted, moreover, that such a foot was an undeniable handicap to a ship's officer, whereas it would be far less a handicap to a leader who did so much of his work in an airplane. In this connection, it would be a handicap only to the leader himself in the event his plane was forced down far from aid. Finally, it should be emphasized that the Byrd who planned the South Polar expedition was a vastly larger figure than the Byrd of earlier years. He had an impressively cosmic grasp of life and events, and a winning humility which struck more than one observer as excellent guarantees of success.

CHAPTER XVI

COMMANDER BYRD TELLS BOB DAVIS OF HIS IMPRESSIONS AS HE FLEW OVER THE DESOLATE WASTES OF THE NORTH POLAR REGIONS

THE effect that he had upon other men is made quite plain by an interview which Bob Davis, mentioned earlier in this narrative, had with him about this time.

"What were you thinking about," Davis asked, "when you crossed the Pole (the North Pole, of course) in the air?"

From then on, the dialogue, as set down in the New York *Sun's* column, Bob Davis Recalls (reproduced here by special permission), goes:

For one transitory second the eaglet folded up his wings and dropped his fine dark eyes in humility.

"Do you really want to know?" he answered, lifting his glance and recovering his calm. "I have not been asked that."

"Do you mind?"

"No!" And then the real Byrd cast off his armor of reserve and addressed the earthbound. "I thought of the infinitesimal proportions of mortal man, of the frailty of the atoms that occupy the spaces, of the limitations of those who have taken over the conduct of civilization. I caught for the first time, as in a flash of understanding, the inadequate results of the effort to solve not only the enigmas of space and duration but the problems of mankind.

"At any point of the earth's circumference, at a given elevation, human vision encounters its limitations. The telescope amplifies a definite point, but the whole field of visibility, discernible to human eyes, is comparatively restricted. Beneath me lay a vast, silent, unoccupied field of snow and ice, varying in tune but without life. My knowledge of what existed beyond at every degree of the circle, plus my imagination, carried me into the temperate and tropic zones, the peopled spaces, the seats of empire, the scenes of turmoil, and conquest and the survival of the fittest. I saw armies and navies beyond the fringe of that Arctic wilderness, over which a metal mechanism by man was plunging onward.

129

"I thought of the beginnings; the primitive past, the gradual development of man, the widely separated units that preyed upon one another, the readjustments that took place and of which no records remain. At that time the passing of one group or another was of small significance, in no wise affecting the world as a whole. The little peoples were too far apart to feel the consequences of the minor obligations. Slowly, out of the chaos, the units became interdependent, the races began to unite, the responsibilities of each increasing as the mutual interests expanded. Figuratively, the world became smaller and the sword longer. Each unit began to feel the effects of conflict. The gaps between the countries disappeared; the strong came to the weak and possessed them. Foreign armies conquered other lands. Flames were visible across the seas.

"War, destruction, hatred took the saddle at the peak of civilization. To-day a shot fired in any country is not only heard but felt around the world. The distant tread of soldiers shakes the whole globe, saps the vitality of every nation. . . .

"We have come through the ages worshiping in our different ways the Supreme Being that best suits our multiplied faiths, but the sum total of our occupation of this shrinking planet is a pitiful demonstration of weakness. It is not the geographical but the moral limitations of the world that must be charted and the really great explorers will be those who find the way to universal reconstruction, the first step in which is the abolition of war and the needless destruction of human life."

He was looking at me quite earnestly now.

"Those were the thoughts that occupied my mind May 9 when I flew over the North Pole and on the way back to my native land."

Such was the far-seeing, humble yet resolute spirit of the explorer who now proposed to embark upon the greatest adventure of his life; and who, over and above that, proposed to take into his keeping, the lives of a body of followers a dozen times greater than he had ever accepted the responsibility for before.

It is only when one understands this spirit, and the great duties with which it was burdened, that one is able to grasp the full portent of the preparations which Byrd was making, preparations no less detailed and complete than the program he had announced earlier.

His sense of responsibility warned him that there should be, and his spirit vowed that there must be, no detail omitted in gathering together the supplies and equipment which would maintain his force while the scientific program was being carried out.

He could count as no more than a small help the experience he had gained in the Far North. The two regions were so utterly different; the Far North a low, level stretch, the Far South a mountainous ice field, full of treacherous crevasses and falls, and ending, on the Pole side, in mountains which were ten and twelve thousand feet high. Of equally little value were the records of previous antarctic expeditions. All earlier explorers had done all their work on the surface, afoot and with dog sleds. Byrd meant to use dog sleds, and his feet would be brought into play, too, insofar as the weak one could be trusted. But the bulk of his major operations would be carried on in the air. And from the air the viewpoint would be so different as to make observations of earlier explorers of much smaller limits.

In order to gain any guaranty of success it was necessary, then, to start and plan from the ground up and he equipped his forces to the last needle.

CHAPTER XVII

"THE expedition," Byrd himself declared, "must have the most thorough equipment. "It would be very easy to go there, get nothing, and lose every man."

First of all, in fulfillment of his contrary resolution to "go there, get something, and lose no one," Byrd obtained four ships. The *C. A. Larsen,* a 14,800 ton whaler, was made available by Magnus Konow, internationally known sportsman and principal stockholder of the Ross Sea Whaling Company. Konow had long been a warm friend and admirer of Byrd. The *Larsen* was an unusually sturdy ship which had been used through a series of summers as a floating base for whaling ships in the Ross Sea. Possession of it helped Byrd solve the problem of getting his enormous stores of supplies down to New

134

Zealand. The *Sir James Clark Ross* was another supply ship.

In addition to these two Byrd had another pair which were put to much harder and more important tasks. The *City of New York* was his main ship of the four. It had been known as the *Samson* when he bought it, and had been in service as an ice breaker. He renamed it in honor of the municipality whose citizens gave him such considerable aid in financing his expedition. It was the *City of New York* which went farthest south. Byrd drove the stout vessel's blunt nose straight through the ice packs below New Zealand, on into the Ross Sea and all the way to the Bay of Whales near which he set up his headquarters which he called Little America.

The fourth ship was the *Chelsea* which Byrd renamed the *Eleanor Bolling,* in honor of his mother. This was the chief supply ship. When the Ross Sea party left New Zealand for the great stretch of ice upon which Little America was established, the *Eleanor Bolling* accompanied the *City of New York* as far as the pack ice, there unloading her supplies and returning to New Zealand from which, in the course of the next

135

year and a half, she made two other voyages southward.

Four ships were three more than any Polar expedition had ever needed. Byrd had, indeed, a small fleet; but the scope of his plans made all four necessary.

There were likewise four planes; three which engaged in numerous observation flights and the giant, three-motored Fokker, The Floyd Bennett, in which the actual flight to the South Pole was made.

Byrd had been careful to find exactly the vessels he needed. He was no less careful to make sure his planes were all they should be. All four were watched with the minutest care while being manufactured. Every smallest part was passed only after the closest inspection. And after they were put together and pronounced ready for use, they were given even more grueling tests. The Floyd Bennett, for example, was accepted for the expedition only after it had been flown 25,000 miles and its efficiency proved beyond the shadow of a doubt.

Every division of the expedition was equipped with the most dependable radio sets. Such radio equipment as the Byrd force obtained was an utterly unheard-of addition to the equipment of any Polar unit. Not only were the ships provided, the ice ship, the *City of New York* and the *Eleanor Bolling* being fitted with powerful, 500 watt intermediate-frequency transmitters, but the headquarters at Little America were similarly provided. There were, in addition, three short-wave transmitters for the three major divisions of the Ross Sea group. Finally, each airplane had its own, small portable set. In a sentence, the radio equipment was such as to guarantee that no member of the expedition, if cut off from the main party, would be left without efficient, adequate means with which to communicate his plight and summon aid.

A curious, though somewhat less sizable piece of equipment made especially for the expedition was a so-called sextant camera, the first of its kind. This was constructed to take pictures while the plane in which it was installed raced through the air at 100 miles an hour. The pictures took in a width of ground eight miles across. No number of airplanes, which could have been transported into Antarctica, would have been able to cover so much territory that the observers would have been able to note and map the conformation of the entire region centering upon Little America. With the sextant camera, however, the several ships in Byrd's expedition were able to photograph, accurately and in detail, and to bring home records of more country than had been charted by all the other polar expeditions.

The sextant camera was the invention of Commander M. R. Pierce of the United States Naval Air Station at Lakehurst, N. J., who developed it in coöperation with the Eastman Kodak Company at Rochester, N. Y. It made 100 separate pictures off of one roll of film and each picture was automatically rolled out, cut off, and deposited in a safe, dark-box attached to the camera.

Notwithstanding that ships and airplanes were to play such a major rôle in the expedition, Byrd had to have a great pack of Alaskan sledge dogs and it was of the utmost importance that these be of the best breed and quality. He ended up with almost a hundred, beautiful, intelligent animals. Each was a cross of a domesticated breed with the northern dog, variously known as malamute, Eskimo, Siberian, or Labrador dog. The domestic strain endowed the animal with intelligence and devotion to its master. The northern strain bred resistance to cold and made what would otherwise have been an ordinary dog into ninety pounds of fighting devil.

Footwear was an important item. It was finally decided to have reindeer boots and these were made of huge sizes, to leave room for the almost unlimited pairs of socks without which no foot could have kept warm. It was necessary, also, to have place for a quantity of senna grass which absorbed moisture. Socks or no socks, feet could not have been kept warm in the sub-frigid temperatures of Antarctic if they had been in the least degree damp from perspiration.

Ships, planes, cameras, radio, footgear, were a few of the thousand and one details which could not be overlooked. In the end Commander Byrd and his assistants found they had remembered everything, but the amount of money they had spent was staggering. Although they had received gift equipment and stores equaling in many instances the value of the stuffs they purchased, they found, while the start of the expedition was still several months away, that their expenditures and commitments had run close to a million dollars, and they were forced to conclude that before they got home from the Far South they would have spent considerably more than a million.

No such total had ever been reached by any previous expedition. Some of the items which went to make up the total were: equipment, $435,000, including ships and airplanes; salaries, $90,000; transportation, over and above the transportation provided by the ships of the expedition, $237,546; dogs, $3,500; sleds and harness, $300; that special footwear, $5,000; books, $1,000; scientific instruments (most of which were donated), $5,000; tents, $1,000; tractors and similar heavy equipment, $30,000; foodstuffs, $30,000.

For all these properties and provisions Commander Byrd managed to find the money, working ahead, slowly but surely, with that dogged refusal to admit failure which had marked his whole career since the day when that undependable foot of his set in motion the curious train of events which tripped him up at regular intervals for years. True enough, his road now was easier than it had ever been before. He knew so much more; his prestige, enormously increased, was a valuable and helpful factor. Nevertheless he did not work without obstacles and disappointments in his way.

CHAPTER XVIII

DEATH OF FLOYD BENNETT A TERRIBLE BLOW
TO THE ADMIRAL; CONTRIBUTIONS OF MONEY
AND EQUIPMENT RECEIVED

UNDOUBTEDLY the greatest shock to the Admiral in the course of the whole undertaking was the death of Floyd Bennett, who had flown with him to the North Pole, and across the Atlantic to France, and who had been named as second in command for the Antarctic expedition. Bennett was the temperamental opposite of Byrd, lovable because of his impulsiveness where Byrd was lovable because of his deliberate thoughtfulness. It was impulsiveness and his kindly feeling for any in distress which cost Bennett his life.

In the midst of the preparations for the Antarctic expedition, three flyers set out from Europe in the plane, Bremen, in which they proposed to make the difficult east-west crossing of the Atlantic. They were the Irish Major Fitzmaurice, and two Germans, Captain Herman Koehl and Baron von

Huenefeld. They got as far as Greenly Island, in the Gulf of St. Lawrence, where their plane in landing, was seriously damaged.

A thousand American pilots were willing to transport repairs, but Bennett would not have been Bennett if he had not volunteered and got under way ahead of all the rest. He reached Murray Bay, Quebec, and there developed influenza. That went so swiftly into pneumonia, despite Bennett's strong constitution, that his case was hopeless. He died, on April 25, 1928, in the Jeffrey Hale Hospital in Quebec. This notwithstanding an eleventh-hour gallant dash by Colonel Charles A. Lindbergh with a serum with which it was hoped to save his life.

By Bennett's death Commander Byrd lost a friend whom he could not well replace and a co-worker whose loyalty and capacity had been proved in innumerable emergencies. That the loss was one which he had never remotely anticipated made it the more severe. It was, indeed, the most severe blow which could have fallen on him.

And it came at a time when he was pressed, not only by the problems of his preparations, but by a curiously embarrassing situation outside of these.

Great Britain had looked for some time upon

the Byrd expedition with a somewhat apprehensive eye. Great Britain had sent her own explorers into Antarctica and while they had not precisely gone over the region which Byrd proposed to cover in detail, nevertheless, Great Britain considered that their explorations gave her a more than tangible claim to much of the territory. But with Byrd about to set off, it appeared that a more exact explorer might make a more calculated claim to these same lands in the name of the United States.

It was a difficult state of affairs. Great Britain wrote the Washington Government. The United States wrote the London Government. It was impossible for Byrd to forecast the final step. All he could do was push ahead, despite his best friend's death, and hope that no insurmountable obstacle would develop.

Perhaps fortunately, in these and succeeding months, he was encouraged by such evidences of financial support as had never been accorded any previous project of the sort he was planning. Deprived of Floyd Bennett, embarrassed by a diplomatic situation which was not of his making and about which he could do nothing, it must have been comforting in a measure to receive the whole-hearted support which was given him.

When his need of funds was most evident the National Geographic Society sent their check for $25,000 and later a second one for a like amount. Colonel Charles A. Lindbergh, far less rich then than he has since become, contributed $1,000. Amelia Earhart, herself a trans-atlantic flyer, having no money of her own to give, consented to indorse a product in order to raise $1,500 which she promptly handed over to the Byrd finance committee. Theodore Roosevelt, III, grandson of President Roosevelt, worked and got together $10 for the explorer he so much admired. Eugene Tunney, not long before crowned heavyweight champion of the world as a result of that famous battle in Chicago, gave $1,000. To pick these out for mention is, of course, only to name a few of the better known contributors. Others, who gave no less generously, numbered in the thousands. It would be impossible to name them all, but a partial list, made up of persons who gave anywhere from thousands of dollars down to only one were printed in the press at the time.

As the time for the departure came nearer, it was discovered that notwithstanding all the gifts

Dr. Buckingham (*Center*), Veterinarian in Charge of Seventy-Nine Huskies That Sailed on the *C. A. Larsen* for the Bay of Whales

© *Underwood and Underwood*

THE FORWARD DECK OF THE WHALER C. A. Larsen SHOWING THE KENNELS OF THE HUSKIES ON THEIR RETURN FROM LITTLE AMERICA

received, there would still be a deficit. It was not Byrd's way to delay the start. He chose rather to go and take his chances. But since the business of collecting funds must still go on he asked his friends to form another committee which would act for him in his absence.

The Byrd Aviation Associates for the Byrd Antarctic Expedition was in consequence formed. Charles Evans Hughes, one time Republican candidate for the Presidency of the United States, more recently Chief Justice of the Supreme Court of the United States, agreed to act as chairman. The remaining members had names hardly less distinguished. They were Vincent Astor, J. D. Barnum, Bernard M. Baruch, Paul Block, Charles V. Bob, John McE. Bowman, James I. Bush, Newcomb Carlton, Harry Chandler, John Chevelier, Richard E. Danielson, Robert Daniel, Raymond B. Fosdick, Artemus L. Gates, Harry F. Guggenheim, George R. Hann, Richard F. Hoyt, Otto H. Kahn, L. F. Loree, Seth Low, Clarence H. Mackay, William H. Todd, Phelps Newbury, Thomas B. Pratt, Joseph Pulitzer, George Palmer Putnam, Julius Rosenwald, Thomas F. Ryan, Donald W. Ryerson, Richard B. Scanderett, Jr.,

145

Oscar W. Solbert, Percy S. Straus, Philip T. White, Theodore F. Whitmarsh.

There was, in addition, an Advisory committee made up of Rear Admiral William A. Moffett, Chief of the Bureau of Aëronautics of the Navy; William P. McCracken, Jr., Assistant Secretary of Commerce for Aëronautics; Edward P. Warner, Assistant Secretary of the Navy for Aëronautics, and F. Trubee Davison, Assistant Secretary of War for Aëronautics.

CHAPTER XIX

THOSE who aided the Richard E. Byrd Antarctic Expedition by contributing to its finances would have made a considerable army if they had been marshaled into a column of squads such as the Commander had drilled back in the days when he directed the training of the Rhode Island Naval Reserve. Those who stood clamorously ready to aid the expedition by contributing their services would have made almost two armies. They came by the thousands.

A fairly accurate check, made a little over a month before Byrd left his headquarters in New York City indicated that not less than fifteen thousand men and women—young, old, middle-aged and in at least a couple of instances octogenarian —had offered themselves for the journey into the Far South. Since the expedition was only a little more than twelve months in the making this meant that applicants came along at the rate of thirty a day. Making allowances for Sundays, holidays and such they must have in reality come in on a work-day average nearly half as large again.

It was an extraordinarily heterogenous procession, the one that filed day in and day out through the Commander's offices. It was made up not only of persons of both sexes and all ages. It was made up of persons from every walk of life and every occupation. By watching it one could measure the universality of that emotional reaction, known as the love of adventure. Rich men, poor men, beggar men—well, if not thieves, certainly doctors, lawyers, merchants, chiefs, all were to be found in the line, each of whose units paused enthusiastically at headquarters, made a hopeful speech and, for the most part, passed disconsolately back to the humdrum job he had hoped to escape. Few of the men had any chance at all. And of course the women had no chance. You would have thought the women could not have failed to see that there was no place for even one of them in such a party as was being organized. What woman could have withstood the rough life, the cold, the rigors of the Antarctic? Neverthe-

148

less there were many women in the enthusiastic line. Bored rich ones who were prepared to finance most of the expedition, provided a place in it was found for them. Hero-worshiping young ones, who no doubt visioned themselves as ministering angels. And, it must be confessed, a few silly ones who seemed to see in Commander Byrd a sort of super matinée idol. These last got scant consideration. Nor was it possible to give the others much more. They might be no end worthy, as regards intentions, but time simply was not available to give them more than the briefest sort of inspection as to qualifications.

"Awfully sorry, but we have no place for a woman. No, we can't use a dishwasher. Our dishwashers must be six feet tall, and be able to lick their weight in icebergs if not in wildcats. Mending? Madam, we'll do our own mending or wear 'em ripped. Oh, you're as strong as a man, are you? And used to all sorts of hardships? Went hiking for a full month in Yellowstone Park last summer, did you? Well, even at that we haven't any place. Awfully sorry."

If this isn't a verbatim report of what was said in the Byrd headquarters a dozen times a day it is, at least, truthful as to spirit. And it was not only in the office, with the applicant standing across the desk, that it was said. The same sort of speeches were made over the telephone. They were made, even, on the street, for more than one dogged candidate refused to take the first "No!" and waylaid the Commander or one of his aides at the most strategic corner.

The men whom Byrd finally chose for his staff were, one and all, picked men. Picked for their jobs. Picked for their physical perfections. No man with a flaw had a chance to break into the select crew, nor half a chance. Nor did it matter if the flaw was hidden, for Byrd did not rely upon his own ability to hunt it out. He did set himself up as a judge of such characteristics as personality, temperament and temper, sociability and such. But when it came to deciding whether the candidate had the proper reflexes, good eyesight, no diseases, he called in the best doctors he could find. That meant the best in the country, for without going outside the lists of those who had volunteered to join his party he could have found an examining board second to none.

This being true, it will be readily seen that there was no place among the stokers of his steamship for the ambitious young helper in an ice-cream factory who volunteered to shovel coal. There was even less place for the earnest, but utterly unprepared clerks who marched bravely forward, hunching up their narrow shoulders to make them seem broader and stronger prompted by the spirit of adventure.

How successful the examining board was in weeding out the unfit, is evidenced by the fact that when the expedition left Little America more than a year after it arrived, its numbers were intact, and more than intact—in healthier condition, for the most part, than when the long, wearing labor started. It is, of course, axiomatic, that work improves a strong man, where it wears a weaker one down.

Resolute as he was about refusing any save the fittest men, and men only for his expedition, Byrd was equally firm in refusing the myriad luck pieces, charms, emblems, badges, insignia and talismen with which well-meaning admirers would have cumbered him. He could not have helped being happy to find so many people eager to bestow the blessing of good fortune upon his enterprise. But on the other hand he could not have begun to take the array of offerings that were made. In the end, he accepted only two. One

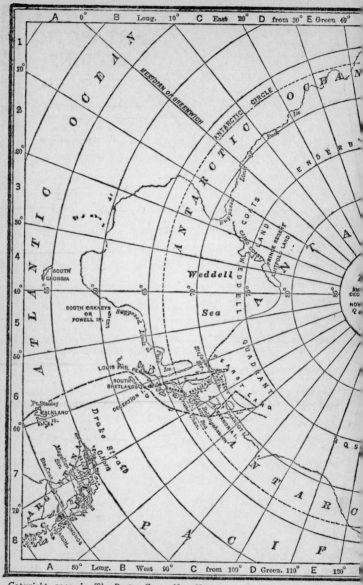

THE LATEST CHAN

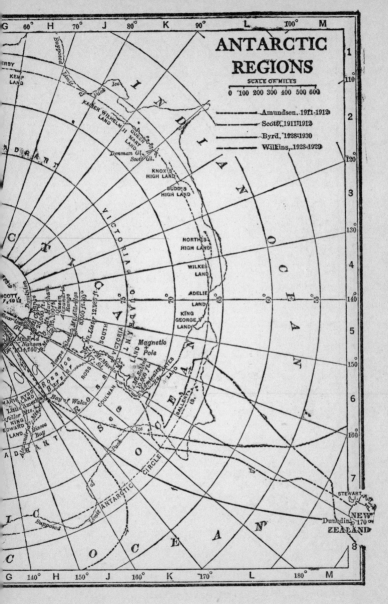

ANTARCTIC REGIONS

was the pin of his fraternity, Kappa Alpha (South); the (South) being necessary because in the Civil War that national college brotherhood had split irrevocably. The other was the blood and fire flag of the Salvation Army, which came into his hands with the blessing of Commander Evangeline Booth, and with her Godspeed upon his perilous adventure. These two were presented to him shortly before his chief ship, the *City of New York,* sailed from New York City. All the others, insignia, emblems, dogs, portable houses and what not, he refused, gratefully but firmly.

Shortly after Byrd's selection of a Boy Scout to accompany the party, the selection being the result of a national competition which was won by Wagle Scout Paul Siple, possessor of fifty-nine merit badges, the Antarctic expedition made the gesture which definitely indicated that its long, rigorous travail was begun. The date was August 26, 1928.

CHAPTER XX

THE STOUT SHIP, *City of New York,* STARTS FOR
NEW ZEALAND, NINE THOUSAND TWO HUN-
DRED MILES AWAY

ON the afternoon of that day, the first section
of the exploration party left New York in the
City of New York for the under side of the world.
The *Eleanor Bolling,* being a steamship, was able
to start later since it was not dependent, as the
City of New York was, upon sails and sails alone.

The largest city in the world made a public
event and more of the ice-breaker's sailing with
the first of the Byrd men who were not to return
from the cold Ross Sea for more than a year.
Dignitaries attended the departure, and the citizens turned out in multitudes. They filled the
streets, they thronged the pier by thousands and
thousands. And when the low, puffing tug
hauled the *City of New York* out into the East
river a shout swelled up that all but silenced the
whistles that shrilled in endless succession on the

155

shipping massed along the water front. It was a departure invested with as much pomp and dignity as had attended the triumphant home-coming of Colonel Charles A. Lindbergh, after his nearly miraculous crossing of the ocean the year before. It was, in short, as impressive a maritime ceremony as the city had ever seen.

The *City of New York* did not get away until late afternoon, but preparations had been going strenuously forward since early morning; and even at noon there was no cessation in the hurried loading of the last of the great stores which crowded the stout ship's dark hold. Down there, up to the last minute, most of the thirty-one members of the exploration force who sailed on the *City of New York* worked shoulder to shoulder, begrimed and weary, but happy, too, in the thought that their great adventure was at last begun. It was, parenthetically, as odd a crew of workers as ever got together in the bottom of a ship. Side by side with old salts, and husky stevedores, labored the sooty, sweating sons of some of the proudest families of the country, men who had volunteered for the enterprise and had been delighted to get taken on and obey orders, whatever the task.

As the hour for starting drew on, friends and relatives of the crew and of the expedition force invaded the ship for last farewells. And when these had been said, the visitors packed the tug *Macon,* New York City's municipal reception boat, as guests of the city, and in it kept pace with the slowly moving expedition ship down the river and through the lower harbor, waving farewells again.

The *City of New York* was a rare sight as her sails got up and she began to glide along under her own power past Fort Hamilton, past the Statue of Liberty, and on toward Ambrose Channel. Any square-rigged sailing vessel is a rare sight in New York harbor in these days of steam; but the *City of New York* had been especially prepared for the occasion. Her sails were spotless. Her stout sides were gleaming white from the coats of paint newly brushed on. Her metal work gleamed immaculately under the afternoon sun.

As the Battery began to disappear in the faint haze which inevitably lurks in the foreground of the towers of Manhattan, a gray Junker plane came out of the clouds that seemed to have pinned

157

their light draperies to the Woolworth spire. It sped like a racing bird until directly over the sailing ship and then the watchers below saw the solitary pilot's arm signaling his farewell and good luck to be added to the already heaping up well wishing of the multitude on the piers behind. Shortly the Junker was joined by a swift Army plane. And then, for almost a half hour, the two air craft gave an exhibition of dives and slips and spins and hairpin turns high in the air.

The planes continued with the adventurers until the latter had got well on toward Ambrose Channel. The *Macon* continued even farther. It went on and on, urged by the hearts of the friends and relatives it carried. It halted only when in the open sea. And even then it did not turn back, but marked time upon the restless waters until the *City of New York,* moving before a fair wind, was almost hull down, and only its sails and tall masts and spars were clearly seen in silhouette beneath the soft evening sky.

Commander Byrd himself was a passenger aboard the *City of New York;* but he went only as far as Hampton Roads, Va. There, with his wife and son, Richard Byrd also, he disembarked and hurried back to New York City to complete his final arrangements for the rest of the expedition, and for the other ships of his fleet which eventually got away in September.

While the chief of the explorers worked in New York, the sailing vessel which he had quitted, continued sturdily along on its 9,200-mile voyage which was to end at Dunedin, New Zealand. Meanwhile the *C. A. Larsen* got away, and the *Eleanor Bolling,* the former made her way through the Panama Canal according to plan and docked in the Pacific at San Pedro, California. There, on October 10, 1928, Byrd went aboard with others of his force after a swift ride across the continent. A little in advance by now, the *Eleanor Bolling,* commanded by Captain Gustav L. Brown, was plowing through the Pacific overtaking the *City of New York* under the command of Captain Frederick C. Melville.

There followed, for all three ships, first days of warm, pleasant voyaging through the blue tropic seas, and the customary foolery with Neptune when the Equator was reached, then an abrupt change into the cool, blowing space closer to New Zealand. There was a momentary bit of excitement on November 7 when the news of the presidential election came by radio. But for the most part the passage was uneventful save for the inevitable storms.

ENGINEERS OF THE *Eleanor Bolling*

E. J. THAWLEY
Second Asst. Engineer

F. MCPHERSON
Chief Engineer

JOHN CODY
First Asst. Engineer

RETURN OF SOME MEMBERS OF THE BYRD ANTARCTIC EXPEDITION. *Left to right*: DR. VOJTECH,
GEOLOGIST; A. T. WALDRON, CHIEF DOG DRIVER; M. RONNE, SAILMAKER; N. D. VAUGHN, ASST.
DOG DRIVER; W. F. LEUTHNER, GEOLOGIST; C. D. ALEXANDER, SUPPLY OFFICER; ED. GOODALE,

CHAPTER XXI

ARRIVAL OF THE FLEET IN NEW ZEALAND, SOON TO LEAVE FOR THE SOUTH POLAR SEAS

THE slow sailing ship *City of New York* got to New Zealand about the middle of November—last of the fleet to arrive. There were more ceremonies. Red tape was cut for the expedition. Commander Byrd was tricked out in a presentation Maori robe. The *Larsen's* cargo was shifted to the other ships, including the planes, and all her other burden. The whaling fleet with headquarters at Dunedin gave the explorers a dinner. Fresh meats, fruits, vegetables and eggs were loaded; foods needed to minimize the danger of scurvy, most dreaded of all the diseases which threaten explorers of the world's cold places. The pack of sledge dogs recovered in a measure at least from the sickness which had afflicted them as their ship rolled upon a surface so much more unsteady than their accustomed Alaskan snow. A reckless young Czechoslovakian geologist, spend-

161

ing his last cent to catch up with an expedition which had repeatedly refused his services, was finally accepted as a tribute to his persistence. Byrd announced that in honor of Shackleton and Scott, heroes of earlier Antarctic expeditions, he would carry a British flag to the end of the world for which he was bound.

Now it was the last of November. The expedition must be on its way for it was necessary to take advantage of the short Arctic summer, at its crest in December. On November 26 all preparations were ended. A storm threatened and a day was lost, another, and another. Byrd stated that the expedition positively would get off on November 29. This was Thanksgiving day, a proper day for the start. And Byrd was the more urgent because sailors from the whaling fleet reported ice conditions favorable to the south. But on November 30 the ships were still at Dunedin. They were still there on December 1.

But on December 2 they got away. On that day the Commander and a score of his force sailed away on the *City of New York* for their year and a half of travail. Almost, one hears Byrd murmuring to himself, as his vessel gets out of the choppy harbor, "What price an undependable ankle, now?"

The inevitable picture of such a start is of a proud vessel, with all sails set, running fleetly into the open sea before a fair wind. As is so often the case, the fact did not fit the fancy. Byrd and his men sailed well enough. But it was a practical, workaday sort of sailing, such as the exigencies of the situation required. They sailed at the end of a tow rope whose forward reach was tied securely to the *Eleanor Bolling*.

The way of it was this. The weather, while satisfactory, had not brought a proper wind on that starting day. So, rather than lose time, the Commander decided to use the steam power of his supply ship.

For the honor of the ship *City of New York* it must be added hastily that this towing process did not continue long. Shortly the fickle wind shifted and thereafter, at times, the *Eleanor Bolling* was hard put to keep up with the clean-hulled sailing vessel. Indeed, the voyage became a sort of race. There was, of course, never any question about which was the faster. The *Eleanor Bolling* was that, incontestably. But every once in a while, when the wind was right, the crew on the *City of*

163

New York had a chance to cheer as their ship forged momentarily into the lead.

According to plan, the *Eleanor Bolling* was to accompany the *City of New York* as far as the pack ice. There she was to unload her cargo and hurry back to New Zealand. From New Zealand she was to make two more voyages down to the pack ice before the winter set in and the pack froze. Each trip she was to be met by the *City of New York*. That vessel was to take over the latest cargo, push with it through the pack ice to the Bay of Whales and add to the provisions of the Ross Sea party.

The first days of the long voyage—it was more than two thousand miles from Dunedin to the Bay of Whales—were almost pleasant days. Overhead was a hard, bright sun. All around the gray water rolled, but with so little force that it did not seem to threaten. Shortly, however, ice appeared, huge solid chunks against which the *Eleanor Bolling* would have run at considerable risk. The pace slackened somewhat.

Now, too, the wind which had seemed no more than cold outside of Dunedin grew icy. It grew stronger, also, and sent the stout *City of New York's* bow dipping heavily at times into the rising sea. Overhead the sky grew more gray, grew almost black.

Next in order appeared icebergs, lifting their vast bulks up from the water until they towered like white hills. So huge were their shapes that it was difficult to believe twice as much of their total proportions were below the surface.

They seemed harmless enough, the icebergs, but the wary commanders of the two ships gave them wide berths. Under the action of the water in which they float, icebergs often split in twain, and then if a ship is too near the resulting waves may do no small damage.

After the two ships had been out two weeks the ice pack came into sight, and this was a most curious spectacle. It might have been land, that ice, snow-covered land, with a broken edge at the water line. It looked solid enough, and it was solid. But it was also undependable. Sometimes it held together all of one piece as far as the eye could reach. Then again it parted here, there, in a dozen places, opening up long leads wide enough to permit a ship to pass.

The *City of New York* hove to off the pack, took over the *Eleanor Bolling's* cargo, and after that stout steamer had swung around for New

Zealand, awaited a propitious lead. That opening coming a week or so before Christmas, in she plunged. Followed such sailing as no one ever had done before. A mile and the lead ended. A patient wait, or a bit of pressure and it was open again. A few more miles. More waiting. More effort.

Christmas day was spent in the ice pack, but it was a jolly Christmas nevertheless, with plum pudding, and presents for every one, and over head the antennæ of an ever ready wireless picking up stray bits of news, and sending out brief word of the party's well being. Checking the force at its merrymaking, noting every one in health, one can be sure that the Commander was now doubly glad he had been so insistent upon physical perfection when he selected the sixty odd men of the Ross Sea force back in New York.

After Christmas, the ice opened again and more miles were gained. Shortly, then, they were through the pack and out into the comparatively open waters of the Ross Sea and the Bay of Whales.

CHAPTER XXII

ARRIVAL AT THE BAY OF WHALES AND THE
FAMOUS ROSS ICE BARRIER

THE Bay of Whales is a fortunately situated body of water which lies between the pack and the solid field of ice known as the Ross Ice Barrier, in honor of the man who discovered it. The Ross Ice Barrier lies to the south of the Ross Sea, an unbroken stretch of solid ice reaching back to the true land of the Antarctic. It was on this shelf, in the spot to be named Little America, that the expedition was to live for the long months of its stay at the bottom of the world.

For generations the Bay of Whales has been a haven to explorers following frost-bitten noses down over the rim of the world in search of the South Pole. Weary and blizzard-blown, they have sailed their ships into its safe, quiet reaches with sighs of relief.

Perhaps that "quiet reaches" goes a little far-

167

ther than the facts warrant, since even in the Bay of Whales the winds are mighty, the cold is so intense that the inert ice keeps up a constant noisy snapping of protest, and lunging floes and other dangers are too frequent to permit of real quietude in any visitor. But comparatively speaking it is an accurate description. All around the winds are far wilder, the cold is terrific and the dangers more numerous. Reflecting upon what they know they will find outside, explorers are well content with the Bay of Whales.

They are doubly content, since the region is one in which they have no right to look for any kind of a bay at all. To make a bay you must, if you go by the usual rules, have water—and land.

Water there is in this part of Antarctica in quantities to float the world's fleets. But of land there isn't enough to make a city lot, unless you go straight down. Instead, there is the largest fixed field of ice known to man; and it is upon the northern face of this that the Bay is found. There, in the vast Ross Ice Field, the combined force of wind and currents and tides have contrived to dig out a small shelter in which a man may safely pause to catch his breath before starting on the final dash toward his southernmost goal.

The Bay of Whales is, in a manner of speaking, a bay within a bay. The Ross Ice Field itself is the immovable cover on a gulf so mighty that by comparison, the Bay of Whales becomes a water of Lilliputian proportions. The Bay could float many fleets, but fleets might well be lost in the vast extent of water which lies beneath the Ross Field. That is upwards of four hundred miles along its north-south line, and almost as wide.

The field lies free on the north. Only the Ross Sea is there. But to the west and south and east it is locked fast to solid land. On these sides its borders are such peaks as Mounts Terror and Erebus, the Prince Albert Mountains, Mount Discovery, South Victoria Land, Mount Markham, Mount Christ-church, Queen Alexandria Range, Queen Maud Range, Mount Nansen, Charles Bob Mountains, Marie Byrd Land, The Rockefeller Mountains, Cape Colbeck, Alexandra Mountains and King Edward Land.

These, through the ages, have formed an immovable barrier against which the Antarctic winds have year after year flung the ice pack which gathered and took form out in the restless waters

to the north. With the coming of each new summer and the brief northward movement of the
pack, much ice was always left behind. This slow
but constant addition is what has formed the Ross
Ice Field. Every twelve months the border of the
field has gone a little northward, until now it ex-
tends almost a half thousand miles outward from
the mountains which fringe the Polar Plateau.

It is only recently that explorers have under-
stood the true character of the field. Not so long
ago they looked upon it as no more than an unusually sizeable floe. They thought that, like all
other floes they had seen, it floated free upon the
sea. Whenever they ventured upon it they went
in constant apprehension lest, like other floes, it
should go to pieces under the stress of a storm.

This was the view of even such contemporary
authorities as Scott and Shackleton. It was not
until Raold Amundsen put in months of pains-
taking investigation that the contrary was discovered to be true. Amundsen, checking his own
findings with previously puzzling observations of
earlier explorers was able to declare that his fore-
runners had been mistaken. "The field," he wrote,
"is in reality firmly wedged upon the solid rock
of some great, immovable land."

Amundsen's conclusion must have been a pleasant extra reassurance to Commander Byrd on that day in early January, 1929, when he set about establishing himself and his Antarctic forces of some sixty men in a permanent base after the grueling voyage down from Dunedin, New Zealand. For quiet and secure though the Bay of Whales was, by comparison with the region all around, it was so only by such comparison. Compared, on the other hand, with such an anchorage as the harbor of New York, or of New Orleans, it amounted to just about nothing at all. Seen from the *City of New York,* even with the optimistic eyes of Byrd's force, it could have seemed no more than a precarious niche in a wall of ice so high that its crest towered over the ship's tallest spar.

Year after year the driving force of wind and currents have piled the Ross Ice Field high and higher. Everywhere its level is well above the surface of the water. In most places it rises a hundred feet or more; in some more than two hundred, and from these several elevations it stretches back, rough and treacherous beneath its deceiving covering of snow, until it locks into the land.

The Bay of Whales constitutes a more than ordinarily favorable landing place because there the face of the barrier, instead of being high and precipitous, is low and gently sloping. Even at the border of the Bay, however, the landing is by no means easy. For one thing, floating ice, no less than the constant danger that a mountainous piece of the cliff will scale off, makes it impossible to run a ship in close so that stores can be put off as at a wharf. Instead, with the vessel anchored at a safe distance, every box, every pound of provisions, every animal, every piece of equipment, must be sent ashore in small boats or dragged toilsomely from ship to shore on pull-ropes over a wide stretch of ice-filled sea.

This was the arduous labor which the men of the Byrd expedition had to perform that cold January in 1929 before they could even think of establishing their base. In a temperature so low and sleet-filled that every rope on the *City of New York* was fattened by ice to ten times its original size, they struggled with the great engines of the plane in which Byrd was to fly to the South Pole, with tons and tons of provisions and fuel, with sections of the houses which they would build

172

later, with equipment and supplies of all sorts and shapes and weights.

Even at that they were not wholly secure. Their ship was far enough from the gleaming wall of ice to be in no jeopardy, but on more than one occasion, while the ferrying of goods was going on, men all but lost their lives as a bit of the barrier unexpectedly gave way. Once thirty were within a foot of death because a great section of ice flaked off as they worked just back of it. It was just such an accident as this late in January which gave Commander Byrd the opportunity to save the life of Benjamin Roth, one of the aviation mechanics with the expedition. Byrd went headlong into the sea when a piece of the barrier broke away and carried Roth down with it. Only his swift action saved the life of Roth. Incidentally, it was only the prompt action of other men of the expedition, in getting both Byrd and Roth into warm quarters, that kept both from pneumonia.

It was a forbidding world into which Commander Byrd took his men, in more ways than one. But for the novices of the party, at least, it was a world whose amazing variety of interests far outweighed its challenge. Above everything else, these new men, or for that matter all the men, were struck by their environment's bewildering beauty.

The common conception of Antarctica is of a dull dead white country. Beautiful, perhaps, if a monotonous blanched purity can make for beauty, but having a weary sameness in which ever direction the eye might turn. The fact, however, is wholly to the contrary. Antarctica is, in truth, everything but white. It is a world of color, intensely vivid. And this is so because the utter absence of dust allows the brightly shining sun to play upon ice and snow with well nigh unbelievable polychromatic effects. Consider this sunset, described by Sir Douglas Mawson in his *Home of the Blizzard,* published by J. B. Lippincott Company of Philadelphia.

"The widening spaces of the zenith," he writes, "are azure; and low in the north they are emerald. Scenic changes are swift. Above the mountain plateau a lofty arch of clear sky has risen, flanked by roseate clouds. Far down, the south is tinged with indigo and ultramarine, washed with royal purple paling into cold violet and grayish blue.

"Soon the north is unveiled. The liquid globe has departed but his glory remains. Down from

174

the zenith his colors descend through greenish blue, yellowish green, straw yellow, light terra cotta, to a diffuse brick red; each reflected in the dull sheen of the freezing sea. Out on the infinite horizon float icebergs in a mirage of mobile gold. The Barrier is a wall of delicious pink overlaid by wondrous mauve. . . ."

Azure. Emerald. Purple. Blue. Yellow. Green. And mobile gold. It was in such a riot of color as this that the men who had sailed down in the *City of New York* worked at times and considered it far more than casual compensation for the risks they took in portaging their goods from sea to shore.

CHAPTER XXIII

THE BUILDING OF LITTLE AMERICA, BYRD'S BASE FOR MORE THAN A YEAR

IT was a magnificent setting for the structure which Byrd now, in early January, 1929, began to rear as a headquarters for the extraordinary tasks which were to engage himself and his men for more than a year. And in its way this structure was, if not as magnificent, certainly only a little less remarkable considering the conditions under which it came into existence. It was a great and complicated effort, involving scores of men, days of rigorous labor, and a wealth of material; and the important circumstance never to be forgotten is that all the material used—every stick, every nail, the smallest machine—had been transported thousands of miles, under conditions which had frustrated men who earlier had tried to work out similar plans. Not until Byrd came into the struggle was any one able to carry such a plan through to completion.

The main problem, naturally, was that of sheltering the men of the Antarctic party so that they might be able to carry out the scientific program which was, of course, the rock bottom reason for their presence in the distant, beautiful, but forbidding region. It was a problem which involved health and comfort too, up to a point at least; but above all it was a problem which depended for its solution upon speed. Painfully difficult though it was to work in the bitter temperatures of Antarctica it was necessary that no time be lost. Once Byrd had moved with slow observance back from the edge of the ice cliff to a spot where he felt able to say, "Start here!" work had to go forward at a gait no less rapid than it would have gone on a summer day back in the States. No delay could be permitted. Everything had to be finished before the winter solstice set in with the long months of darkness.

No delay was permitted, and in an incredibly short time there was set up, upon the rough level of the Ross Field, such a village as never before had been seen below the Antarctic circle, the largest, and the most nearly complete and best equipped community that ever had been built in the Polar regions. The completeness of the com-

177

munity is a point to be stressed, because Byrd had emphasized it from the very beginning. That had been his thought even back in 1927 when the whole project had only begun to take shape in his mind. His expedition, he said then, was to be (and it was) the first of its kind able to rescue itself if rescue became necessary. No such catastrophe should overtake his party as had overtaken Umberto Nobile, the Italian explorer, who lost so many men after his dirigible was wrecked on its flight into the Far North.

The final result of the Commander's resolution back in 1927 was this, that in 1929, although his expedition was 2,300 miles from any civilization, and although he was for months so situated that no relief force could get to him, he was at all times in a position to send relief to any of his men who came to grief. This, the Little America built upon the Ross Ice Shelf made possible.

Little America, broadly speaking, was made up of three clusters of buildings set within a circle rather more than a thousand feet in diameter. The circle was far enough back from the edge of the cliff to guarantee that no segment of it ever would slide off into the sea while the men of the expedition worked, or worse, slept. It was near enough to the edge to provide for the shortest possible haul of extra provisions which the *City of New York* would bring from time to time.

The *City of New York,* while the Little America colony set about constructing their quarters and workshop, had faced about and started back for Dunedin. It was part of the program that the ship should make two more round trips from New Zealand to the Ross Field with the extra provisions which the ice party would need during the severe winter, when it would be impossible for the stoutest ice-breaking ship to drive through the impassable winter pack.

This is primarily a narrative of Commander Byrd and of what he and his men did in the tiny community they set up at the edge of the South Polar Plateau, about 800 miles from the Pole, but it would be far too incomplete if no mention were made of the labors and sacrifice of the other men of the expedition whose rigorous efforts aboard the *City of New York* made the accomplishments of the main party possible. The struggles of these men reached a climax on the second voyage back from the Ross Sea. Months later, landing ahead of the Main Byrd party at San Francisco, Lieut. Harry Adams described the heart-breaking fight which the scanty ship's crew waged on that occasion against hurricanes, mountainous waves and sleet.

The run down from New Zealand had been difficult. Winter was in the offing and the temperature fell steadily; and, since winter in the Antarctic means also storms of such intensity as are unknown elsewhere, a mad sea was added to the terrific cold. The run back north, however, was immeasurably worse. In the few weeks that had elapsed since the start from Dunedin, winter had come in its full fury.

On the very day that the *City of New York* turned away from the Bay of Whales she had to break through floes which had already begun to freeze together in great mile-wide barriers. Almost overnight, there threatened such a disaster as had overtaken Sir Ernest Shackleton in the Weddell sea fifteen years earlier. Shackleton's description of the freeze-in which eventually resulted in the loss of his ship, is the virtually perfect account of such a calamity. Except for its disastrous conclusion it is, too, a virtually accurate account of what befell the City of New York in her northward struggle. The story is told in

*South,** the remarkable narrative of Polar adventure which Sir Ernest Shackleton published in 1920. The expedition was completed in 1915, but the book was delayed by the World War.

"It was often necessary," Shackleton wrote, "to split floes by driving the ship against them. This form of attack is effective against ice up to three feet in thickness.

"When the way was barred by a floe of moderate thickness we would drive the ship at half speed against it, stopping the engines just before the impact. (The *City of New York* carried an auxiliary engine as well as sails.) At the first blow the *Endurance* (Shackleton's ship) would cut a V-shaped nick in the face of the floe, the slope of her cutwater often causing her bows to rise till nearly out of the water, when she would slide backwards, rolling slightly. Watching carefully that loose lumps of ice did not damage the propeller we would back off two or three hundred yards. She would then be driven full speed against the V, taking care to hit the center accurately. At about the fourth attempt, if it was to succeed at all, the floe would yield. A black

* The Macmillan Co., publishers, New York, and reproduced by permission.

sinuous line, as though pen drawn upon white paper, would appear ahead, broadening as the eye traced it back to the ship. Presently it would be broad enough to receive her and we would forge ahead. In this way the *Endurance* would split a two or three-foot floe a square mile in extent."

How the men aboard the *City of New York* must have watched for that "black sinuous line," which told them they were able to go a little farther! How apprehensive they must have been when it failed to appear according to expectation! For its absence was a threat that, like Shackleton's party, they might be frozen in through the whole winter and, like Shackleton, might be compelled to stand by and watch the floes crush their ship when the warming winds of summer broke them apart and the wild winds tossed the fragments one upon the other.

"The roar of pressure could be heard all around us," Shackleton wrote in describing the destruction of the *Endurance,* a destruction which the *City of New York* narrowly missed. "And I could see, as the day wore on, that the lines of major disturbance were drawing nearer the ship. . . . I could hear the creaking and groaning of her timbers, the pistol-like cracks that told of the starting of a trenail or plank, and the faint, indefinable whispers of distress. . . .

"At seven P.M. very heavy pressure developed with twisting strains that racked the ship fore and aft. The butts of planking were opened four and five inches on the starboard side, and at the same time we could see from the bridge that the ship was bending like a bow under titanic pressure. Millions of tons of ice pressed inexorably upon the little ship that had dared to challenge the Antarctic.

"A strange occurrence was the sudden appearance of eight emperor penguins from a crack a hundred yards away at the moment when the pressure upon the ship was at its climax. They walked a little way towards us, halted, and after a few ordinary calls proceeded to utter weird cries that sounded like a dirge."

If it was a dirge that those penguins sang, it was fitting music, for in those moments the *Endurance* was irrevocably broken, though the final crumbling of the small challenger of the Far South was delayed for a few hours. Of that dénouement, Shackleton wrote:

"The ship was hove stern up by the pressure, and the driving floe, moving laterally across the stern, split the rudder and tore out the rudder post and stern post. Then, while we watched, the ice loosened and the *Endurance* sank a little. The decks were breaking upwards and the water was pouring in below. The twisting, grinding floes were working their will at last with the ship. It was a sickening sensation to feel the decks breaking up under one's feet, the great beams bending and then snapping with a noise like heavy gunfire.

"The water was overmastering the pumps, and so to avoid an explosion when it reached the boilers I had to give orders for the fires to be drawn and the steam let down. The plans for abandoning ship in case of an emergency had been made well in advance and men and dogs descended to the floe and made their way to an unbroken portion of the ice without a hitch. Just before leaving I looked down the engine-room skylight as I stood on the quivering deck and saw the engines dropping sideways as the stays and bed-plates gave way. I cannot describe the impression of relentless destruction that was forced upon me as I looked down and around. The floe, with the force of millions of tons of moving ice behind was simply annihilating the ship."

CHAPTER XXIV

BYRD'S SHIP, THE *City of New York*, IS SPARED
THE FATE OF SHACKLETON'S SHIP, *Endurance*

It was exactly such an annihilation that the *City of New York* faced on that final, dauntless drive northward. And she too felt an ever thickening belt of ice about her.

To break this, and to send the ship crushing through the pack which grew more and more solid, was the unceasing effort. Once all movement was stopped. The ice was too thick to be broken forward. It was so close behind that there was no room even to back up and make a running try. What happened to save the situation, as Lieutenant Adams relates it was little short of a miracle. There came a half gale from the south. For a space, floe and ship moved northward together before the tremendous pressure of the fortunate wind. Then, abruptly, the strain upon the floe became uneven and it gave way along that line which had previously been weakened by the

185

ship's blows. The "black sinuous line" for which all were watching appeared. It broadened. It became a wide lead, a lane through which the *City of New York* raced with all sails set and her engines pounding furiously while all on board held their breath, or nearly so, until the pack was at length cleared and the open sea was ahead with no more to menace them than an occasional iceberg.

While the *City of New York* was undergoing the adventures which culminated in her all but hapless fight with the floes, Byrd and his men were getting Little America in order, were setting up those three clusters of buildings which were to be their homes and workshops for twelve months and more and were equipping them.

Of the chief cluster, the Administration Building was the principal building. Besides living quarters for a number of the party, including Commander Byrd, it contained the radio laboratory, the dispensary and the radio reception room; and attached to it were the meteorological shelter and the pilot balloon station. Several hundred feet south from it, but still in the same cluster, was the absolute physical house, and in between was the observation igloo. This last was one of the few buildings of Little America made of ice.

Directly behind the Administration Building, that is to say due north, were the medical stores house and the building which contained the food supplies, these two being separated from each other to minimize loss in case of fire. It was, indeed, the factor of fire which was largely responsible for the separation of all the main buildings from each other.

Beginning at the Administration Building and running back beneath the snow, was a tunnel. This continued westward a thousand feet or so, to the second cluster of buildings. Chief among this group was the Mess Hall. Here were more living quarters, a radio station, a storehouse and a photo-laboratory all under one roof. The Mess Hall was, moreover, the center, roughly speaking, of a triangle whose three points were represented by the three radio stations which carried the antennæ that kept the Byrd expedition in touch with the world. A little distance away were the quarters for the dogs, and the sledge repair and blacksmith shop. Eastward, were the snow flyers' garage, the taxidermy station, the dog maternity ward, the seal chop house (where seals were butchered) and the seal cache.

The third cluster of buildings was due north. It comprised the aviation repair shop and the gasoline cache.

The whole constituted, by and large, a by no means comfortless community. The quarters were small, but they were far more commodious than most of the men had expected, and no one was known to complain. On the contrary, there were frequent murmurs of satisfaction, especially about the warmth. These were especially noticeable after some one had come in from a tramp, or a piece of work in the sub-zero temperatures outside.

The warmth was in no small degree due to an ingenious idea of the Commander. He hit upon the notion of having the doors of the huts (constructed of course in the States) built like the doors of a lock. Under his plan there were two doors for every entrance and one could not be opened until the other had been securely closed. Thus there was no chance for a cold wind to pour suddenly into a room; and this was vital in a region where a wind often raced at a speed of more than 100 miles an hour upon temperatures of fifty and sixty below.

The walls of the living quarters were also built

for warmth, with several thicknesses of wood, and insulated with material having ample air spaces to check the cold. The windows were few and all had three panes, one back of the other. To some degree these stopped the light. But on the other hand the air spaces between the thicknesses stopped the cold, which was much more important. Finally, there were no eaves upon any of the roofs of any of the buildings. This was in deference to the fierce winds that blew so often. Eaves would have given these a too excellent finger-hold. With such a grip, they might have ripped a roof off as easily as a man lifts the cover from a pasteboard box.

Once the matter of house construction had been finished, and even before it had been fully completed, Commander Byrd set some of his crew at the task of building a runway for his planes. He got about this work all the more quickly because he was tremendously eager to get as much exploration work as possible done before the winter darkness.

A runway was necessary because the surface of the Ross Field, even after the snow had been scraped down to the more or less solid ice, was far too rough to permit a plane to take off. The labor of smoothing down a lane wide enough and long enough to get the planes safely off the surface was a tremendous undertaking, and when it was completed there was the unending job of keeping it in shape. The crew of sixty men which made up the expedition party was little enough.

Nevertheless, the tasks set were completed in due order and with no great loss of time. This is attested by the chronological record of Byrd's performances.

January 6, 1929, one finds, is the date upon which the party was established in Little America (not completely established, naturally, but certainly settled); for, coming to January 16, one finds the record:

"Commander Byrd successfully completes his initial flight in Antarctica, obtaining photographs from his airplane of 12,000 square miles of territory."

On January 31, the work of exploration was interrupted by that rescue of Roth, the aviation mechanic who fell into the Bay of Whales. But by February 18 the risk of pneumonia was so small that Byrd was up and doing again. For that date we may put down the entry:

"Commander Byrd made his second successful

aërial reconnaissance, and a more important one, exploring more than 40,000 square miles of unknown area."

The next important entry to be made finds Byrd staying home and sending Harold June, Bernt Balchen and Larry Gould out. This was on March 8. Shortly after this, and not very long before the disappearance of the sun and the long winter darkness put an end to such air explorations for a time, Commander Byrd summed up the achievements of his expedition as of that date in a wireless message to Secretary of the Navy Adams. He stated:

"The following geographical and geological report of newly discovered areas is made:

"On January 27, 1929, in the Fairchild plane, The Stars and Stripes, the Rockefeller range of mountains was discovered.

"On February 18, 1929, an aërial survey of this range was made by Captain A. O. McKinley.

"On March 7, 1929, Geologist L. M. Gould, landed in the plane, Virginia, at the base of one of the southern mountains of the range for the purpose of geological investigations and geographical location of several mountains to form base points to make the aërial survey less inaccurate.

"And so, for the first time, aviation has discovered a new land, surveyed it and landed on it for scientific investigation.

"These mountains consist of a group of scattered, low-lying, snow-swathed peaks and ridges. They are irregularly arranged in an arc beginning in Lat. 78 degrees, 14 minutes, S; and Long. 155 degrees, eighteen minutes, W. on the southeast, curving thence toward the east as far as Long. 153 degrees, 25 minutes, W and thence northward where they terminate in Lat. 77 degrees, 47 minutes S.

"The arc reaches its greatest width in longitude 154 degrees. In this part of the group are also found the most prominent mountain masses.

"There are some forty peaks and ridges, only half of which exhibit patches of bare rock. In photographs taken from the westward, from altitude 6,000 feet, twenty insignificant patches of bare rock can be seen in addition to the bare peaks. These rocks appear to be struggling to keep their heads above the snow.

"The highest peaks and ridges are heavily flanked with snow. The remaining peaks, if I may call them such, appear as protuberances or bulges in the snow surfaces. The valleys are partly filled with snow or ice, so that from a plane the mountains do not appear rugged or imposing."

Only a prodigious efficiency could have brought about the completion of so much important work in such a short space of time, and in the face of such difficulties as Antarctica offered.

CHAPTER XXV

JOHN JACOBSON, SAILMAKER OF THE EXPEDITION, TELLS OF KILLER WHALES AND PENGUINS AT DRILL. LIVING CONDITIONS AT LITTLE AMERICA

FROM another source, it appears that work was not the only order of the day. At intervals, it seems, there was leisure in which a sailorman could look around and gather up material for one of those tales which sailormen so love to spin. There must have been leisure, else how could John Jacobson, sailmaker for the Byrd expedition, have had the time to note in such detail the whales of the Bay of Whales?

It would be pleasant to be able to say that John Jacobson was the first to discover the whales in the Bay, and that he christened the harbor. This honor, however, goes to Sir Ernest Shackleton whose ship was so bumped and belabored by indignant mammals the afternoon he first found the shelter that the name sprang to his lips as a downright inspiration. But certainly it can be said that of all the members of the Byrd expedition no one observed the whales so closely as did John Jacobson, especially that variety of whale known as the killer-whale. The killer-whales exercised a vast fascination for John Jacobson. He watched them time and time again. And when he got home he was able to talk about them by the hour. What he said was summarized one afternoon by a reporter for the New York *Sun*.

"Bad boys they are, I'll have you know," the reporter quotes sturdy old John Jacobson. "They have heads like English bulldogs. They are thirty to forty feet long, and the fiercest things that swim the sea. To see them fight with another whale of a different species, probably twice their size, is a terrible sight. They bite big chunks out of the poor creatures and the sea turns red all around the massacre. I've seen them from the Byrd ship reared up six feet out of water, bloody and ferocious, fighting to a finish.

"When killer-whales see a man on the ice they hold a council of war, or a powwow, and they dash themselves up against the bottom of the sheet on which the man stands, hoping to jar him into the sea.

"Believe me, one loses all desire for the society of a killer-whale after seeing him in action. I believe he is the wickedest creature in the animal kingdom. A lion is a lapdog compared to 'em."

Sailmaker Jacobson observed the few other forms of life in the Antarctic, too, and had many interesting comments.

"The seal," he said, "often goes far in on the ice to escape the killer-whales. I have seen seals driven into our camp just like you would herd a bunch of sheep.

"The penguins are funny fellows and great companions. They waddle along, upright, just like dignified old gentlemen. They are very inquisitive, and go around poking their noses, or bills, I should say, into everything. Once in a while they get snubbed. One of them waddled up to one of the huskies and nipped the dog's nose. What happened to that penguin was a crying shame. There were penguin feathers all over the landscape."

Jacobson said one of the most delightful sights of his whole expedition for him was the spectacle of the penguins at drill.

"Yes, drill!" he emphasized. "Every now and then a whole gang of them, maybe six or seven

straight to the Ross Ice Field out of a Chicago meat-packing house."

The whale meat was a welcome addition to the menu of the camp; but even without it there was little lack of variety in the meals served in Little America between January of 1929 and February of 1930. Commander Byrd's endeavor was to give his force substantially the diet they would have had at home, and he came pretty close to doing just that.

As regards vegetables he had almost no problem at all. The World War had taught the palatability of dried potatoes and such so that Byrd's storekeeper felt safe in loading up with every sort of dehydrated product. Beans. Spinach. Potatoes. Apples. Corn. Even cranberries. To these it was only necessary to add water. That, after a few hours, brought the beans or potatoes or whatever it was, back to plump softness. There remained then only the matter of cooking, and this was accomplished to the queen's taste, or by George Tennant, otherwise Gummy-the-Cook, and his two assistants. With a stock of food containing some 1,500 items, and including sixty tons of groceries, five tons of ham and bacon, flour of all sorts, and a multitude of the oddments needed to spice a meal, he rarely saw anything but hungry smiles when his boarders stormed the Mess Hall at his cry of "Come and get it!" or whatever was used as the equivalent of that in Little America.

The force usually breakfasted at six o'clock, a practice which held good even in the months of darkness when there was no very urgent reason why some, at least, of the party should not have kept under the covers a while longer. A typical breakfast consisted of bacon or ham and eggs, griddle cakes, a cereal, and coffee. Yes, there was plenty of cream for the coffee. A powdered cream, which served well enough when mixed with a little water; and water was easy to obtain. Tennant simply filled a can with pure, clean snow and let in melt in the kitchen.

Luncheon was as stout a meal as breakfast, with meat and potatoes and vegetables and bread. Dinner was even stouter. It bulked over luncheon by the addition of a soup and a dessert. The desserts were as varied as Tennant's praiseworthy ingenuity and his almost unlimited larder made possible. Pies. Puddings. Cakes. They came to the table of Little America in all flavors and thicknesses. And, of course, in addition to the staple articles of diet there were plenty of tidbits; mustard for the meat, syrup for the griddle cakes, a jar of jelly now and then. Many a fashionable boys' camp in the Adirondacks has served a less satisfactory collection of meals than Byrd's men got thousands of miles farther away from any grocery store. The Commander believed in taking the best care of his men.

One important item on the menu was the stuff that is looked upon as a luxury, and a fattening one at that, in more civilized regions. There were, for every man on the expedition, a round hundred pounds of candy; roughly a quarter of a pound a day for the thirteen months and a little over of their stay. This ration was a good four times what the party would have averaged back home, but it was no more than enough. The terrific and constant cold of Antarctica compelled every man to maintain in his body an excess of heat far over that which he would have had to maintain in his normal environment, and candy is a great producer of heat.

It is easy to conjure up a picture of the close, but comfortable, living quarters of the Mess Hall and the Administration Building, with resting men sprawled in every available space, a pocketful of candy to munch and a book to read. This is, no doubt, a deceiving picture since it omits to take into consideration the work schedule of the expedition—the geological research, the dredging and delving of the biologists, the explorations completed, the meteorological inquiries, and all. But still, one suspects there must have been a considerable amount of candy-eating and reading in off hours. Certainly there was candy available. Moreover, there were books.

CHAPTER XXVI

A WELL SELECTED LIBRARY OF A THOUSAND VOL-
UMES PROVED A BOON IN ICE-BOUND LITTLE
AMERICA. RADIO IN TOUCH WITH THE OUT-
SIDE WORLD

WHEN the Byrd expedition sailed from New York it carried a round thousand volumes. It was, for the most part, a collection of stories of adventure which the Commander selected to solace his men through the long, inevitably idle darkness. Kipling, London, Dumas, Robert Louis Stevenson, Sir Walter Scott were the chief authors. But there were also Balzac, and Dickens and Conrad, and for the moody-minded there were "My Favorite Murder" and "The Psychology of Suicide."

These were all at hand whenever a man had candy and a few leisure moments. And certainly there must have been leisure after the dark months arrived. In the chronology of Byrd's important undertakings in Little America there are no entries between late March and the middle of October. This does not, of course, mean either that the sun vanished for all that period or that work stopped completely. As a matter of fact, the sun was still a daily visitor in April, and it again became a daily visitor in late August. Moreover, even without the sun, some activity was possible. There were always the twilight hours of noontime provided by the moon.

Obviously, however, no aërial flights could be made, and only the most urgent travel with dog sleds; for even with the aid of the moon the light at best was poor. A dimmish gray diffused through the atmosphere with now and then an aurora flickering faintly and far down, toward the edge of the sky, a northern glow casting an almost imperceptible pink over the few clouds there. There was another, even more important reason why work had to be undertaken with caution. This was provided by the succession of winter storms. These, in their full strength, brought winds that no man could stand against, and such snows as are unheard of elsewhere in the world.

When Little America was first set up on The Ross Field its tiny buildings made black spots visible for miles against the surrounding whiteness. Long before the winter was over, snow had banked and drifted over all save the tallest points. A bit of the roof of the Mess Hall was visible at times. The radio towers managed to get some of their tall, latticed length clear. But the rest of the community was apparent only in the additional unevenness of the snow's surface where a hangar, the dogs' quarters, the Mess Hall, the gymnasium or some other building lay buried.

No small amount of those winter months were lived underground by Byrd and his men, or virtually underground. They went by tunnel from the Administration Building to the Mess Hall. By tunnel, too, they could reach others of the more important buildings. It must have been a curious experience. The mistake must not be made, however, of thinking that it was a silent one in any general sense. To speak of the great white silence of the Antarctic is to use an accepted phrase. It is, too, to use a phrase which is true after a fashion. But while silence broods over the whole of the Far South, each little area is full of its own noises, much as an empty house at night is full of noises. Poking their heads out of doors into the impenetrable gloom of the Ross Field's midnight, Byrd's men would almost have sworn on occasion that they heard birds singing. Sometimes two of them would look sharply at one another in wonderment as their ears caught sounds which were unbelievably like the shrill, sharp cries of animals. At other times there were curious, eerie groans and moans. And even in the locked security of their quarters sometimes they caught a rumbling, rolling murmur which could have been nothing but a trolley car in the distance, except that they were all perfectly aware there were no such things as trolley cars round about. All this magic and more was accomplished by the restless shifting of the ice upon which their houses stood; by this, and by the imperceptible but resistless pressure of the water beneath the ice, and by the fury of the winds which tore constantly at those fortunately eaveless roofs.

It was a magic which might easily have been disturbing had the inside of the Mess Hall and the Administration Building been as dark as the field without. Happily, the Byrd expedition which was setting a record for size and achievements under its ever so faintly limping commander, also set a record with the amount of electrical equipment it brought to brighten its Antarctic home. Electrically, too, the party set a new era in exploration.

With the last of April the sun disappeared, leaving only a meager glint of brightness now and then along the horizon. Inside the huts, however, the first electric generator ever transported into the Antarctic provided a flood of light for all purposes. Living quarters and workshops were amply supplied. Charles E. Lofgren, the storekeeper, checked his goods by it. Tennant turned a switch when he went into his kitchen to prepare a meal.

The spectacle would have made a curious contrast for an older explorer, if one could have dropped in to pay a call, such a man, say, as Amundsen, Scott, or Shackleton. Shackleton, it is true, did have some small electrical equipment, although he writes: "We never could afford to use the lights freely." But the others had been obliged to get along with lamps and candles which flickered all too feebly.

The men of Little America, however, not only had electricity for lighting. They had it for medical purposes too. Doctor Francis D. Codman, chief physician of the party, had brought along two powerful sun lamps, and there was electricity enough to run these. For fifteen minutes each day each member of the expedition had to bathe in the radiance of these. This was a rule which endured throughout the entire winter, while the sun was not present to furnish a natural health-giving light.

The electrical equipment, too, ran the radio; and the radio was another means whereby the Byrd expedition set a record. Other Polar explorers had had radios, but none ever had had such equipment as Byrd took along. So complete was his preparation in this direction that all through his stay in Little America he lived with his finger tip on an electric bell, by which he could practically ring up the entire world. Nothing like it had ever been done before. At virtually a minute's notice he could call New York, South America, Europe, San Francisco, Australia, and almost any spot upon the world's surface he chose to reach. Each day he was able, if he wished, to inform the world of what had happened in the previous twenty-four hours. And this grows into a privilege of astounding proportions when it is contrasted with the long months during which earlier explorers had gone with the world in utter ignorance of their place or actions. For such as these, Polar expeditions meant a complete isolation from civilization. For Byrd it was hardly more than moving into an adjoining room so far as communication was concerned.

By radio, Byrd was able to tell the outside world when he started out dog teams and men to lay supply caches southward in preparation of his Polar flight. He was able to inform his vast audience when the first cache had been set down a hundred miles or so from Little America; when the second had been situated a hundred miles beyond the first; when the third had been established, and the fourth. He was able to let the world know that he was doing this work with four teams of dogs, that each team carried about a thousand pounds of provisions, that Joe de Ganahl was in charge of the undertaking.

The radio served a multitude of purposes. It was available when Byrd wished to have the oath of citizenship given to Carl O. Peterson of the expedition. Peterson desired to become a lieutenant in the Air Corps Reserve, and he was reluctant to wait until he got back to the United States. But it happened that he was not a citizen, and all officers of the United States army must be citizens. It was a regrettable deficiency in his qualifications, but by no means an insurmountable one. Byrd simply sent a message winging through ten thousand miles of space to the Government at Washington. Ten minutes of tapping with a radio key in Antarctica and it was all fixed.

On another, earlier occasion it was the radio which made possible a two-way conversation between the United States and a plane in which Byrd was poised three thousand feet above the icy gray Bay of Whales. So fine was the reception on this occasion that in New York it was possible to catch the drone of Byrd's motor as it spun to keep the plane aloft.

Radio, too, carried amusement and information to Little America as easily as it carried news from Little America to the world. Sometimes a theater would broadcast its program for Byrd's men. One afternoon the crowd gathered around the receiving set in the Administration Building got the welcome word that a supply of athletic equipment was on its way from the University of Pennsylvania to replace an earlier stock sadly depleted by usage. On still another day there came a challenge to a chess game with a Montreal player. The challenge was, of course, promptly accepted and thereafter, each week the move and counter move was thrown into the air for a ten thousand mile journey. That was quite a game. It ran as long as a Chinese play. It ran months.

Once, when Commander Byrd was slightly puzzled about the problem of comfortable sleeping, the radio brought him the advice of experts. By radio, no less authorities than Fitzhugh Green and Captain Bob Bartlett sent suggestions as to how the party in Antarctica could avoid frozen clothes and other inconveniences attendant upon sleeping.

"Lay the snow shoes or skiis next to the ice or snow," they sent word from the easy chairs which they occupied before an open fire in the Explorers' Club in New York City, "then spread a short-haired sealskin or a piece of canvas; then a piece of caribou skin; then lie down with the arms inside the parka and draw an extra skin over you, if you have an extra skin."

One can almost hear Captain Bob Bartlett chuckling at that last clause. One can almost see him unbuttoning his dinner coat under the influence of steam heat and the glowing fireplace in the Explorers' Club and laughing heartily. "That's a good bit," one hears him say. "Repeat that last bit, to make sure they get it. 'If

you have an extra skin.' And be sure to emphasize the 'if.' "

"If you haven't an extra skin," the message of
advice went on, "sleep sitting up. And a most
important item is a long, thorough beating of the
clothes with a light stick or a whipstock upon
first entering the shelter and then again before
lying down to sleep. If using sleeping bags, pro-
gressive disrobing should be followed to avoid
getting particles of snow inside."

CHAPTER XXVII

WINTER DARKNESS DRAWS TO A CLOSE. THE SUN COMES AS A WELCOME VISITOR. PREPARATIONS FOR THE GREAT DAY, THE FLIGHT TO THE SOUTH POLE

EVERY anniversary which arrived while the expedition was at Antarctica was made cheerful by the radio. The day of the anniversary of Byrd's trans-Atlantic flight brought messages of congratulation from all the world. On Easter there was music fitting to the day sent on from New York. On the Fourth of July there were addresses and music. And, finally, it was the radio which told the waiting world that the long darkness at Little America was at an end. This news was flashed out into space on August 25, 1929.

For days it had been imminent. The twilight hours which had numbered less than four in the middle of the long southern night had been lengthening, a little at a time. One week they were five. The next six. Then they were ten, and

213

down along the horizon could be seen for a space each day a promising golden tint. Finally there came a day when the sun itself was actually visible for a minute or so. This was not a true sunrise. It was no more than a refracted portent. But only a little after it appeared, the real orb itself rose majestic and bright one morning above the horizon. The little universe in Antarctica was transformed.

It must have been, for the stalwart crew and the slim, quiet, deliberately gaited commander, a day, a week, of tremendous excitement, that day and week which followed the return of the sun to the vast whiteness which made up the Ross Ice Field. There was, to begin with, the exhilarating change from the monotonous amber glow of electricity inside the houses and the depressing gray blackness of out-of-doors to the prismatic beauty which the new sunlight made of the ice and snow. But there was much more than that. There was, for example, the little thaw which each day of sunlight brought, and the daily revelations of this, the rediscovery of a new roof to break the snowy stretches of Little America. There was release, too, in a physical sense. Now a man could get out to stretch his legs, for the

214

storms, or at least the most terrible storms were past, and one dared walk out in the open. There was work, and that, after the long days of forced inactivity, was a rich, welcome privilege.

Little America became a whirlpool of activity. The biologists began again to send their dredges down to the bottom of the Bay of Whales, three, four, five hundred fathoms, bringing up great hauls of the passively floating or weakly swimming animal life, the plankton, with which the Bay abounded—minute organisms, plants chiefly diatoms and blue-green algæ, and animals largely protozoans and entomostracans, with occasionally eggs and larvæ and a few jellyfish.

The geologists searched assiduously, and such small discoveries as a piece of moss, or a few pebbles, or a shell made a whole day worth while.

The dogs were mad with delight at being free from their winter quarters. They yelped and tugged in ecstasy as they were harnessed again to the sleds.

The photographers brought out their equipment and when nothing better offered took pictures of the penguins imprisoned while awaiting transportation to America; or of the killer-whales

215

which began to push their long, rakish snouts through the rotting ice of the Bay; or of a seal spinning in a frenzy with his mouth full of a half-swallowed fish that would neither go in nor out; or of the airplane hangars and their attendant machine shops slowly emerging from under their coverings of snow.

Around these last the activity was most strenuous. The planes had to be inspected, the equipment had to be gone over, the fuel stores had to be checked. And once more there loomed the Brobdignagian task of clearing a runway from which the planes could take off in safety. A more important task this than it had been even in January, for now, as all were aware, the climax of the whole expedition was imminent.

Back in New York, when his expedition was in the making, Commander Byrd had said that the Polar flight was to be secondary to the scientific work of his party. He meant it then. In a sense it held true throughout the entire period of exploration. But in another sense circumstances would not allow it to remain true. There was a quality of splendid drama about the projected journey by air from Little America to the Pole, which caused it to take on a vast importance

216

in the minds of the world which was watching the little group down in Antarctica. It was becoming, that flight, a symbol of victory. No matter what else might be achieved, there would always be a sense of defeat if the Floyd Bennett, with its three giant motors, failed to carry Byrd in triumph to the southernmost spot on the globe and back.

No matter what Commander Byrd had said in New York, no matter what his common sense told him down in Little America, it is pretty certain that emotionally he reacted much as the rest of the world was reacting. He, too, could not fail to appreciate the drama inherent in the flight which each day now brought nearer. One feels sure that he felt a keen interest in the renewed activities of the biologists, and the geologists; one feels sure that he never forgot the vast scientific importance of the work his meteorologists were doing. But one feels equally sure that in his heart of hearts he felt most strongly about his forthcoming journey by air over the great white waste above which man had never flown before. One sees him most often about the great craft which was to be his vehicle; one hears his voice most often in careful discussions with his aides and his mechanics.

There were still many days before the flight would be made. It was late August when the sun came back and not until late November would the Floyd Bennett take the air on its epochal 1,600 mile journey. But the days were no more than enough for all that had to be done. Those supply caches were still to be placed; one, the most distant by Byrd himself in the Queen Maud Mountains. And the placing of these caches was of the utmost importance. Properly situated, Byrd and his aides would have a chance should their plane fail them and force them down in the Antarctic wilderness. Improperly situated the plane crew might easily perish before help could reach them from the base at Little America.

Besides the supply caches there were a multitude of details to be arranged. Every instrument had to be checked. The provisions to be carried in the Polar flight had to be carefully estimated, so much for immediate use, so much more to have in the event of disaster. The Floyd Bennett's gasoline consumption per mile was known, but perhaps the winter in the Antarctic had altered this. A slight change might be of the greatest moment. A test was imperative. No less imperative were tests of every other working part of the plane. There was, too, the matter of clothing, and the matter of route, and of maps. All these had been carefully considered, but on such a hazardous undertaking it would have been foolhardy not to consider them again, on the chance that some small flaw had been overlooked.

Between August 25 and November 28 there were many days, but no day was anything but full for Byrd and for the men who would make the great flight with him, for Balchen, McKinley and June.

CHAPTER XXVIII

THAT day when the bright sun came back to
Antarctica, Byrd and his men would have taken
oath that no detail had been overlooked to assure
the perfection of the swift Polar flight which
was to be the climax of their long months of
labor, of darkness, of cold. For the flight, no
less than for the more solid but not so dramatic
endeavors performed about Little America, a self-
sustained community had been built where before two frozen huts had never been seen together. A fleet of ships, a corps of experts, an
unmatched mechanical equipment and commissary
had been gathered. To the last minutiæ every
care had been taken to make a perfect foundation
from which to build into the air, to an apex no
less perfect.

Nevertheless, at the last instant, it appeared
that the perfection of the flight was, after all,

to be marred; and by a circumstance so trivial in comparison with the amazing magnitude of the imminent project that one feels sure Byrd must have managed at least one laugh, notwithstanding his tardily discovered dilemma.

This is not, of course, to say that the flight itself was at any time in doubt. Day in, day out, that was irrevocably certain, as certain as it was that the fleet plane, *Floyd Bennett,* with its three high-powered motors, stood ready and waiting in the hangar which made a black dot on the Ross Field's snows; as certain as that the men were ready. Byrd and Harold June and Bernt Balchen and Ashley McKinley were chafing to make the start; as certain was it as that every last ounce of equipment had been made ready, oil and fuel and food for the flight— food, dogs, sled, skiis in the event of the plane being forced down.

But for Byrd it would not have been enough merely to fly to the Pole and return, by plane or by the aid of that long-suffering foot of his, with a pageful of figures as proof. It might have satisfied, up to a point, his personal pride; but at his age and after all he had gone through, there was little of that left in him. He was after a larger benefit. He wanted to go home, to the men of science who had watched his expedition with such hope, and say: "Here it is, as plain as though you had made the flight yourself. Mile on frigid mile! Mountain on snow-capped mountain!"

Other men, the Peary who had been the idol and envy of Byrd's youth, Scott, Amundsen, had come back from one Pole and the other, bringing magnificent pages full of proofs. Of what use to follow them if one brought back no more?

This was the question which made the obstacle at the last. The answer, more than a little baffling, hinged upon a matter no weightier than six hundred pounds. After twelve thousand miles and more of triumphant journeying; after twelve months and more of triumphant struggle, six hundred pounds, representing one photographer and his camera and his food supply, cost Byrd no end of sleep.

To understand why this should be you must know both the limitation of such a plane as the *Floyd Bennett* was, and the nature of the terrain over which the *Bennett* was to fly. The *Bennett* was powerful, and its reliability had been proved by 25,000 grueling miles of test flights, but with the necessary load which it bore on the sixteen hundred mile long flight from Little America to the Pole and back, it could get only so high into the air. Ten or twelve thousand feet represented its ultimate ceiling.

The significance of this is made plain when you learn that ten or twelve thousand feet represented also the ultimate height of the mountain peaks which Byrd's plane had to top if the Pole was to be reached. Ten thousand feet for the plane. Ten thousand feet for the mountains. It was a perfect stand-off. And in such a situation a pound was worth pretty close to a foot. Omit the photographer and his food supply and his heavy aërial camera and you had a virtual guaranty that the *Floyd Bennett* would clear the tiptop peak, even Axel Heiberg Glacier, with a comfortable margin. Add on the photographer, his food supply and his camera and "what have you."

Young Captain Ashley C. McKinley, crisphaired and bright of smile, little less handsome in his fur-collared parka than a movie hero in a drama of the Alaskan snows, was the photographer. And between the day of the sun's re-

© Underwood and Underwood

Digging a Wind Shelter During a Blizzard in the Antarctic

Scene Showing Terrific Ice Conditions in the Antarctic

how many feet of clearance dare we count on when we get to the Glacier? Dare we count on any?"

The decision took more than a day, more than a week, perhaps more than a month. Byrd's lean, handsome face grew more and more inscrutable as he tried to arrive at it. Balchen rubbed his rugged, keen features and frowned. June tugged at the beard he had grown which made him, in his fur-collared parka, look for all the world like an Elizabethan courtier. McKinley tried to look as though he didn't care a whoop or a holler which way the other three made up their minds.

The final decision was, of course, the only possible one. Some one of the consulting three, doubtless, got up from the final conference, after weeks of test flights and arguments, smacked a fist on the table littered with computations, reckonings and such and cried: "I vote for the camera and Mac! What if we do go down. We can't live forever. Let's also go after the pictures."

One suspects it was Balchen who sent his fist to the table, and his cry through the conference room; for despite his sphinx-like countenance

225

which suggests stoicism he is, by all accounts, a merry, reckless individual. And one feels pretty sure that it was June who chimed in to second the motion, rising briskly in the hope that the issue had come to a head. One suspects those two spoke first; for one feels sure Byrd was taking his time to make up his mind.

Byrd's responsibility, it must not be forgotten, was so much greater than the responsibility of any of the others. He bore the burden that a leader cannot shift to other shoulders. His could be no hasty decision, but a grave measuring of safety and danger.

Nevertheless, make up his mind he did, and in favor of McKinley and the camera, on a day that verged into Antarctica's summer. It was a day handsome young McKinley is like to remember long.

Thereafter the business was mainly one of waiting for good flight weather. And the nearer the approach to midsummer the more likely good flight weather became. There were a few false alarms. A few times Meteorologist Henry T. Harrison came back from his observation station to say hopefully: "It looks pretty good." And thereupon would follow a period of excitement which caught every man in Little America. It was not, however, until November 27, 1929, that Harrison brought a forecast which satisfied Byrd.

On that day, he came in to report that while the weather outlook in the immediate vicinity was a trifle discouraging, the possibilities for the area to the southward, above the glacier and the high Polar plateau were excellent. A bright sun, with no clouds of any moment and no fog.

Byrd considered the details of Harrison's observations, nodded, and the troop of mechanics went out to make sure that everything was right, and a bit more than right, with the *Floyd Bennett*.

If the day on which it was decided to take cameraman and camera was a memorable day for McKinley, that night preceding the flight to the Pole must have been even more memorable for Byrd.

Not, of course, that it was really what you would call night. By then the sun was a brightness in the sky for three-quarters out of every twenty-four, and even the remaining six were not what you would call dark. Dim, yes! But a man was easily able to get about in them. In them a plane pilot could easily see, for example, the black tip of a mountain thrusting upward at

227

a height of ten thousand feet. The Antarctica in general and Little America in particular were like that. With them, in the matter of darkness and sunshine, it was either a feast or a famine. But at least it was sleeping time.

One wonders how much sleep Byrd got. Some, certainly, for that rigidly controlled mind of his would order sleep enough to take care of the labor that was forthcoming. But before the order was given it must have been that the Commander lay there, eyes wide open and staring up at the shadowed ceiling of his quarters, going over all the years of his life. It may have been, too, that as he lay there, that foot of his became, for an instant, full of sensation, as though struggling to cry out: "I haven't done so badly for you after all. I've got you this far, and this is a long, long way, let me tell you, Commander Byrd."

The morning of November 28 dawned bright and fair. Harrison, going to his observation station again, found that he had no need to change his forecast. A bit of a storm, perhaps, in the vicinity of Little America, but over southward, above the Polar plateau, promise of the same clear, untroubled sky. And best of all, a following wind for the last half of the return trip.

Harrison's report was dessert for the breakfast which Byrd and Balchen, McKinley and June, sat down to around six o'clock in the morning. Between breakfast and the middle of the afternoon when the *Floyd Bennett* was actually to rise in the air there was barely time enough for all that had to be done. The plans and preparations had all been completed weeks before, but there were last minute details and vital ones.

Toward noon or a little past, the mechanics— and you may be sure Byrd and Balchen and June were with them—went into the hangar to give the plane its last servicing. It had been kept warm, especially the engines, by small stoves whose heat was gathered into hoods which covered the three motors. Now the gasoline tanks were filled with fuel which also had been warmed. The oil tanks were filled.

Under Byrd's watchful eyes, a man tested all the controls, turned the two wheels right and left and watched the ailerons to make sure they answered; checked the depth controls, the flippers which enabled the ship to get elevation or lose it; worked the rudder back and forth and looked closely to see that the rudder responded.

Byrd, Balchen and June, all three, went over

the instruments on the dash, the altimeter, the compasses, the air speed meter, the three tachometers, one for each motor, the temperature gauge for the oil, the fuel gauge.

The afternoon sped along. Byrd, his countenance set into that mask of immobility which changes so startlingly when he smiles, could find nothing more to do. McKinley, smiling at his beloved camera, was all wrapped up and ready to go. His last glance had been to the aperture in the bottom of the plane through which his apparatus would catch its impressions and that was clear and unobstructed. June, his dark beard resting in sharp contrast upon the light fur of his parka collar, was eager to get at the controls. Balchen was close by, bright-eyed from anticipation. The dogs were in, the dogs upon which they would put so much reliance in case the reliable *Floyd Bennett* failed them. The dog sledge was in, and skiis. Food was in, several bundles of it.

Byrd nodded, and the motors were started. There were nine hundred and seventy-five horse power in the three motors; five hundred and seventy-five in the big center one; two hundred in each of the two on either side. They gathered speed slowly; only gradually were they brought up to their number of revolutions per minute which spelled their maximum efficiency. Once there they ran wide open and in perfect unison. The last testing was done.

Byrd nodded again, and the plane was rolled swiftly out of doors, to the runway which had been newly smoothed across the ice of Little America. A shout went up from the men of the expedition who were not fortunate enough to be making the flight. They formed a semicircle about the plane, a fur-clad booted crew who shuffled excitedly in the snow. Behind them the small houses of Little America seemed suddenly large and enormously safe and inviting. Such few farewells as men are likely to utter under such circumstances had already been said.

CHAPTER XXIX

AT LAST THE TAKE-OFF. THE *Floyd Bennett*
GRACEFULLY LEAVES THE ICE RUNWAY.
SIXTEEN HUNDRED MILES OVER BRISTLING
ICE ENCRUSTED MOUNTAIN PEAKS

BALCHEN was in his pilot's seat first, his hands
going to the controls as though made for no other
use. June, then McKinley who looked down to
make sure that his camera was just as he had
last seen it three minutes before. Byrd got in,
turned, faced the men of Little America, and
smiled so that his usually quiet face was suddenly
alive and bright. His hand raised. Balchen
opened the throttles of all three motors as one.
And in a roar which drowned the last, shrill
shouts from the men who had been left behind
the quartet of adventurers were off. Now, and
no mistake, they were going to find out whether
their ship could get above the Axel Heiberg
Glacier with that extra six hundred pounds. And
trailing behind them was the antenna of the wire-

less outfit with which they intended to tell the
men left behind how the going was.

To the background, loudest of the group which
cheered them forward, was the man who would
help in the telling. He was Russell Owen, staff
correspondent of the New York *Times,* later to
win the Pulitzer prize for his work as the first
Polar reporter, work which was held to be the
outstanding journalistic achievement of the year.
Owen had become Byrd's close friend when he
was assigned to cover the Commander's North
Pole expedition. He was the one man for the
duty, when Byrd looked about to find a reporter
who should accompany the Antarctic unit.

Southward from Little America the course of
the *Floyd Bennett* ran, for some four hundred
miles, above the Ross Ice Barrier. So far an
easy course. The Barrier varied in height above
sea level between two hundred and four hundred
feet. Its surface was jagged underneath its
smooth covering of snow, but no one of the four
in the plane had any thought that it would be
necessary to land, so the threat below them was
no threat at all. An easy course, they all agreed.

Once in the air, Balchen got the feel of his
ship and noticing that it was slightly tail-heavy

reached back over his head and gave the stabilizer adjustment a turn or so. The plane leveled off beautifully. She was flying on an even keel. Above, the sky was as cloudless as Harrison had predicted, and as clean of fog. McKinley, looking around occasionally from his rearmost place to smile a reassurance at the dogs nervously crouched in the plane's tail compartment, though it was just about as comfortable as Little America had been. As a matter of fact, he reflected, it was a lot more comfortable than Little America had been in that period when the Commander was deciding whether the cameraman and the camera could be taken.

Of course there was the noise. The three motors roared so that conversation was next to impossible. The three propellers screamed as the plane bored through the clear air, above the glistening snow, under the bright sun. The feet of the four men felt the whole ship quiver with the vibration.

Byrd, the navigator, bent over his instruments, or stood erect to take a reading with that bubble sextant which he had himself invented for just such a service as this. At intervals he signaled the pilot. Sometimes this was Balchen, some-

234

times June. The two changed at intervals.
Whichever was at the controls veered ever so
slightly right or left in response to Byrd's indicating hand.

But right or left, always the plane thrust steadily into the south. A sizable opposing wind had
sprung up, as Harrison had forecast. "A tail
wind when you come home," he had said, "but
a head wind for at least part of the trip out."
It was not, however, a wind of dismaying proportions and the *Floyd Bennett* drove through
it at a hardly diminished speed.

Slowly, surely, altitude was gained. Despite
a load of more than twelve thousand pounds they
went up, a thousand feet, two, three, four, five,
six. Now Balchen was at the controls and June
was as close as he could get to the engines, smiling to himself as he failed to catch the faintest
break in their even, deafening roar.

They were up to seven thousand feet, eight,
nine. Byrd was moving incessantly, now on one
side of the ship, now on the other, taking those
observations which kept the course true. The
gasoline fumes grew rather unpleasant; all the
more so since, now they were so high up, the

air was thin and breathing would have been difficult even under more favorable circumstances.

Now they were up to ten thousand feet and a trifle over. The mountains were in plain sight, and the higher because, looking backward, they could see the low Ross Ice Shelf. Suddenly the air, broken by the peaks they were approaching, became bumpy, full of pockets, and the strong cross-currents began to jerk and toss the ship.

All the while McKinley had been photographing with that amazing camera of his which could take in an eight mile wide surface. He got pictures of the flat ice field, of the mountain side, of nearly every mile of ice and snow that they passed.

And then, in a moment, they all realized that they had come to the time when they would discover just how high the *Floyd Bennett* could go with twelve thousand pounds aboard.

They were squarely into the pass through which they hoped to get by the Axel Heiberg Glacier.

Abruptly they perceived that their computations had been built a little too much on hope. Balchen, at the controls, shouted "Dump something!" Byrd, who took his time deciding matters when there was time, but who could make up his mind

in an instant, made it up instantly now. It had
to be either food or fuel that they dumped.

"Throw out that bag of food!" Byrd ordered,
and out it went. After all, food was not an item
of immediate importance, whereas fuel was vital.

The plane rose instantly. The situation would
have been perfect, except that there was another
mountain peak, a trifle higher, just ahead. Balchen looked back for a brief instant. No need
this time to cry "Dump something." Nor for
Byrd to make up his mind. His mind was already
made up. He had his hands on another bag of
food and over it went, whirling down to land to
sink deeply into the snow of the mountain top
as the Bennett lifted beautifully and got over the
high mountain with three hundred feet to spare.

McKinley, busy with his camera, had no time
to wonder whether his presence was going to
bring starvation to the party. Balchen had no
time, either. He was busy leveling his plane off
for the last half of the outward flight. June
was busy, too. Those dark whiskers of his
parted neatly in the wind of the propellers as he
leaned forward to smile at the even, unbroken
roar which beat into his cold ears. Byrd, one
feels sure, gave the matter no thought either. In

the way of commanders he had put it cleanly out of his mind on the day he decided that the trip would not be worth while unless the cameraman came along.

As suddenly as they had run into the rough currents of air about the glacier they ran out of them. The country over which they traveled seemed for all the world the same country over which they had traveled before the mountain masses had risen in their faces. The same bright air, the same bright snow beneath, the same bright sky above. The only difference was that its level was some ten thousand feet higher.

The plane was, in fact, soaring above the Polar Plateau, that vast, high table, unknown to any save a handful of intrepid men, which keeps locked in its icy center the intangible thing known as the South Pole.

McKinley, looking around occasionally from his photography to smile a reassurance at the nervous, crouching dogs, was enormously pleased with the ease and comfort of the trip. How very much more comfortable it was, he thought, than Little America would have been with him there and this swift plane going on its way without him.

The *Bennett* had lifted up from Little America shortly after three o'clock in the afternoon. She had flown under the bright sun for almost ten hours. She had covered more than seven hundred miles, and the sun was still a helpful light. Ten hours! More than seven hundred miles. Byrd began to take his bearings with extra care.

Things seemed always to happen swiftly on that trip. Suddenly they had swept into that rough and rending whirlpool of air above the glacier, suddenly they had swept into a smooth, level course again. Now they were on top of the goal toward which they had looked through long tedious months in Little America.

For minutes Byrd had known they were virtually upon the imaginary line which was the object of their quest, and he had signaled their situation to the other three tense men in the *Bennett*. All were expecting the moment of arrival. Yet, when the moment came it was unexpected, and in a way incredible.

It was incredible because nothing happened, and to the mounting imagination of every one of the four it seemed impossible that there should be no explosive occurrence to mark the climax which had been achieved so triumphantly. Yet

239

there was nothing. A moment before the plane had been soaring smoothly over a smooth field of snow. It still soared and the surface below was as even, as smooth as before. Nor was there any sound to mark the event, save the continuing roar of the motors.

Byrd checked and rechecked the plane's position to make doubly sure that the true goal had been reached. Twice and a third time, Balchen swung the *Bennett* in a great circle whose center, provided the navigator's reckoning was correct, and it was, must be the South Pole.

Then, with that curious sense of unbelief a little abated, they started back on their eight hundred miles to Little America. Ahead of them were some nine more hours of flying, and these were to include a halt for fuel just north of the mountain barrier over which the plane had got in that last, nimble rise. The plateaus under them lay as white and smooth as ever. The plane roared along. Balchen still worked the controls. June, with his whiskers still parted by the propellers' gusts, still listened to the sweetly throbbing motors. McKinley continued to swing that fine camera of his for still another and another picture.

© *Underwood and Underwood*

WELLINGTON, N. Z.—SOME OF THE STAFF OF ADMIRAL BYRD ON RETURN OF S.S. *C. A. Larsen* FROM LITTLE AMERICA

President Arosmena of Panama, Admiral Byrd and U. S. Minister Davies, on Return of the Admiral from New Zealand to the Canal Zone.

The mountains came into sight. As suddenly as before, the *Bennett* was buffeted by angry cross-currents of air over that jagged mass of rocks which Amundsen had called the Devil's Ball Room. The Axel Heiberg Glacier came close, but this time it seemed far less ominous. This time there was no need for Balchen to cry: "Throw out something!" The plane, lighter by many gallons of gasoline, rose like a lark to the morning sky. The topmost peak far below, it soared away toward the level spaces of the Ross Ice Field.

There was yet to come the brief landing for fuel, but that was over in such a short time that afterward it hardly figured in the recollections of any of the four. Up again, the plane soared along a course which ran a little eastward of the line which marked the outward flight. North and westward, then, the *Bennett* sped until below Byrd sighted the dog trail a half hundred miles from Little America. He nodded to Balchen and the latter moved his controls. The *Bennett* began to slant down a little.

On that last stretch of their flight they literally coasted home, and blowing them at an even faster gait was that tail wind which Harrison had promised. Already the wireless, with its thread of antennæ trailing rearward, had sent word of the triumph back to the base. Already Owen had relayed the word back to the bigger America.

Byrd, drawing his shoulders together a bit inside his great fur parka, put his sextant down, turned away from all the instruments he had used to keep the true course. Beginning back at the start in Little America, he began to count. The ship had got off a little after three in the afternoon. It would land again at a little after ten in the morning. Nineteen hours in all. In nineteen hours he had completed a journey which Amundsen had not been able to make short of fifty-three days. By this second swift dash he had become the only man to fly around both Poles.

The great adventure was over. And if Byrd, clambering wearily out of his plane at Little America, felt more regret than triumph his mood is easy to understand. The dream is so often so much more absorbing than the reality. Reality means conclusion. It was not only the adventure that was finished for Byrd. Everything was completed upon which he had ordered his days for weeks and months and years. Until he found himself a new dream his searching mind would be at loose ends.

For the moment the one important move was to get aboard the *City of New York* and go back home to find out what the people there thought about the whole achievement.

The fate which had smiled so warmly all the while the expedition was at Little America made the voyage on the *City of New York* an easy one. That same ice pack which a year before had all but locked the ship in through a long winter opened a free road now and the passage through the pack was made in a matter of thirty-eight hours. The whalers at Dunedin, hearing the time, declared it was a record. No ship had ever before got through the ice pack in such a short time.

The people of New Zealand smiled and looked upon this last kindness of the Antarctic as a gesture for which they could claim some special measure of credit.

Now months had passed since the Polar flight, eaten up with the final preparations for departure from Little America, by the long run up to New Zealand which followed that brisk passage through the pack, by all the labor incidental to refitting both the *City of New York* and the *Eleanor Bolling* for the lengthy voyage from New Zealand back to the United States. December was gone, and January, February and March, and most of April. It was the last week in April when the Governor General of New Zealand, Lord Bledsoe—after an intensive round of festivities—bade Byrd and his men farewell, and Byrd replied:

"I would rather say au revoir to New Zealand than good-by, for I am looking forward to coming back again. There is one thing I have never sufficiently emphasized, and that is the great debt our expedition owes to the New Zealand men who volunteered to get our ships south for us. There was not one of them who did not show himself a gentleman. Each man played the game and worked as one of us."

This was Rear Admiral Byrd speaking, for by now the United States Government, in recognition of his remarkable feats, had conferred the higher rank upon him. The new title had one curious aspect; for it could be called nothing short of curious that this constituted a high promotion in that service which fourteen years before had decided that Byrd and his undependable foot could no longer serve it.

Doubtless Byrd thought of that; though of evidence that he did there is none. He wore his new uniform with plain pleasure when he placed a wreath on the cenotaph at Parliament House in Wellington, where the New Zealanders had erected their country's chief memorial to its World War dead. After his long sea trip from New Zealand to Balboa, he wore it in the same simple spirit when he arrived at Panama.

Panama was a resting place. The recently made Rear Admiral arrived there aboard the steamship *Rangitiki,* with Russell Owen, Lloyd Berkner, Charles E. Lofgren, William C. Haines and Richard Konter of his personal staff. The others of the expedition were coming on the slower *Eleanor Bolling* and the *City of New York.* Byrd had hurried on ahead because he felt he needed a rest before the tumult of welcome of which he had been warned awaited him and his men when they arrived in the United States. That rest he proposed to secure by hiding away in cooler Boquette in the Chiriqui Mountains at "Pop" Wright's ranch where he arrived on May 20, 1930, and left on the 23rd to await the arrival

245

of his ships. This was the same retreat which Colonel Charles E. Lindbergh had sought after a somewhat similar experience with admiring countrymen. There he could live quietly for a time before beginning the last stage of the journey home in the company of all his force. It was a pleasant interlude, made all the more so by the cabled announcement that the House of Representatives of the United States on May 16th, 1930, had voted special Navy medals for both himself and the members of his expedition in honor of their achievements.

On May 26 Admiral Byrd completed for the National Geographic Society at Washington, D. C., his condensed story, which was taken by Dr. R. Y. Hildebrand of the editorial department of the Society aboard the *S.S. Santa Ines,* sailing for New York May 27, 1930.

CHAPTER XXX

THE AUTHOR'S SUMMARY OF DATA, THE FLIGHT
TO THE SOUTH POLE, AND RETURN. FUR-
NISHED BY THE NATIONAL GEOGRAPHIC
SOCIETY, WASHINGTON, D. C.

MOST prominent among the societies which
contributed to the Byrd Antarctic Expedition and
conspicuous among all the contributors, whether
individuals or organizations, was The National
Geographic Society. That body, always keenly
interested in any exploration, watched the progress
of Rear Admiral Byrd's project with an especial
attention, and wrote in admiring terms concerning
the most dramatic of the several important feats
which now stand to the credit of the man who
commanded at Little America. Following is a
summary of the data sent to the publishers of
this book by the Society.

It is a striking coincidence that Byrd and his
men entered the ice pack, on their way to establish their headquarters on The Ross Ice Field, on

the seventeenth anniversary of Raold Amundsen's discovery of the South Pole. And as all know it was Byrd's successful negotiation of the pack, and his equally successful establishment of his base at Little America which made his own flight to the South Pole possible.

The then Commander, following his months of preparations and wait, got under way to the South Pole the instant that favorable weather was reported following, of course, the arrival of the most suitable season of the year. With the receipt of word from the meteorological party that the outlook for sunshine up on the Polar Plateau was excellent, the big monoplane, the *Floyd Bennett,* got off without difficulty.

Her load was roughly 15,000 pounds, and this included her four passengers, Commander Byrd, Bernt Balchen, pilot; Captain Ashley McKinley, aerial photographer, and Harold I. June, radio operator and volunteer mechanic. Notwithstanding this heavy burden she flew easily across the piedmont ice, sighting the Gould observation party 304 miles to the southward.

It was shortly after passing this party that the airplane met, and triumphantly passed, the test of tests. This was the crossing of the mountains.

The unusual load was a great handicap; and the last to be added weight, represented by McKinley and his camera and the necessary emergency equipment, lowered the flying machine's ceiling by a clean 1,000 feet. Whether or not this reduced ceiling would be sufficient to permit the airplane to get over the mountains was a momentous question as Byrd and his comrades approached the towering barrier at the point which seemed to offer them the least danger.

Right and left rose frowning cliffs and ice-clad walls. The most nearly safe lane was straight forward, and even if a safer had offered at the last there was no room to wheel the ship. The *Bennett* had to lift itself or crash. That she did lift herself was little short of a miracle. But the indomitable struggle for elevation, the unterrified defiance of gusts, swirls and eddies of air which at times threatened to twist the airplane in two, the reckless willingness to sacrifice possible future safety by casting overboard bundles of provisions, the alertness of mind which suggested the expedient of pouring gasoline into the tanks and lightening ship by throwing overboard the empty containers—these won in the end.

It should be noted, however, that success was

not sure until two 125-pound bags of concentrated food were jettisoned. These gave the vitally needed several hundred feet of extra ceiling, and with a scant few feet to spare the *Bennett* soared out toward the vast Polar Plateau, itself a region of tremendous heights, ranging from 7,000 to 11,000 feet.

From then on every mile of flight added to the airplane records of the Antarctic. To the westward was discovered a great mountain range seen previously by neither Amundsen, Scott or Shackleton. The position of this was ascertained by dead reckoning, by sun compass reading and by sextant observations, as were the positions of all other landmarks.

When the airplane reached the South Pole, the four men in it stood gravely at attention while four flags were dropped. First to go reverently from the side of the *Bennett* was a silken American flag, weighted with a stone from the grave of Floyd Bennett in Arlington Cemetery. This was dropped in honor of the man who had flown to the North Pole with Commander Byrd and who would have also flown with him on the southern venture had he not given his life to aid flyers in distress. Next went a Norwegian flag in honor of Raold Amundsen who had discovered the South Pole and who later gave his life in the search for the Italian, Nobile, and the latter's men in the Arctic. The third flag was the Union Jack, let down in honor of the valiant Robert F. Scott who also attained the Pole but who died on the exhausting journey northward to his supply base. The last flag was that of the French Republic. This was dropped by Byrd in grateful tribute to the nation which had received him so warmly at the end of his flight across the Atlantic Ocean.

ADDENDA

1928

August 25—The sailing vessel, *City of New York,* leaves New York City.

October 10—Commander Richard Evelyn Byrd and his personal party leave Los Angeles for New Zealand aboard the whaling ship, the *C. A. Larsen.*

December 2—The *Eleanor Bolling* and the *City of New York* sail from Dunedin, New Zealand, for the Ross Sea in Antarctica.

December 14—The *City of New York* alone begins its drive through the ice pack toward the Ross Ice Barrier. The *Eleanor Bolling* turns back to Dunedin, New Zealand.

December 25—Commander Byrd and his Antarctic party reach the Ice Barrier in the Ross Sea aboard the *City of New York.*

1929

January 6—Commander Byrd establishes his permanent headquarters, Little America, on the Ross Ice Shelf just in from the Bay of Whales.

January 16—Commander Byrd successfully completes his initial flight in Antarctica, obtaining photographs from his airplane of 12,000 square miles of territory.

January 31—The Commander saves another life, rescuing Aviation Mechanic Benjamin Roth from death in the Bay of Whales into which Roth fell when a piece of the Ross Barrier broke off into the sea.

February 18—Commander Byrd made his second aërial reconnaissance, and a more important one, exploring more than 40,000 square miles of unknown area.

March 8—Harold June, Bernt Balchen and Larry Gould, co-pilots, fly from the base at Little America to the Rockefeller Mountains for geological specimens.

March 19—Commander Byrd flew to investigate the failure of Balchen, June and Gould to return and found their plane smashed.

March 22—Commander Byrd and the three

luckless members of the geological party get safely back from the mishap on the Rockefeller Mountains.

October 15—The supporting sled party moves southward to lay auxiliary supply bases for Commander Byrd's use on his South Pole flight in the event his plane is forced down.

November 4—The geological group begins a 400 mile journey with dogs and sleds to the Queen Maud Mountains to the south.

November 10—The supporting unit comes safely back to Little America after successfully laying supplies.

November 18—Commander Byrd, flying beyond the farthest point reached by the supporting party, succeeds in laying a supply base in the Queen Maud Mountains.

November 28—With three flight companions, Commander Richard E. Byrd, chief of the Byrd Antarctic expedition, begins his long, hazardous flight from Little America toward the South Pole.

November 29—Commander Byrd returns to Little America after completing his South Pole flight, the first man to fly around both ends of the earth.

December 5—On another epochal flight, Commander Byrd locates, explores and photographs 35,000 miles of unknown territory, including a new mountain range.

December 21—In response to a nation wide appeal, Herbert Hoover, President of the United States, commissions Commander Richard Evelyn Byrd a Rear Admiral in tribute to his important work in Antarctica and elsewhere.

December 26—The geological party of the Byrd expediton discovers a cairn containing relics deposited by the Raold Amundsen party eighteen years before.

1930

January 19—The geological group, returning from an exploring trip in the region of Mount Nansen to the south, reports the discovery of valuable coal deposits.

February 7—Sailing down from Dunedin, New Zealand, the *City of New York* drives southward through the ice pack in the Ross Sea and reports her imminent arrival to the Byrd party at Little America.

February 18—The *City of New York* arrives in the Bay of Whales to take the Antarctic group of the Byrd expedition aboard.

February 19—The Byrd expedition quits Little America, and starts back to Dunedin aboard the *City of New York*.

After days of splendid and hearty welcome of the people of New Zealand Lord Bledsoe, Governor General, wishes the Admiral God-speed for a safe voyage home.

May 14—Admiral Byrd arrives at Balboa, Canal Zone, on *S.S. Rangitiki*, and awaits the members of his Expedition for the last lap, Panama to New York.

May 26—Admiral Byrd completed for the National Geographic Society his condensed story.

May 27—Dr. R. Y. Hildebrand of the Editorial Department of the Society takes the Admiral's story to Washington, D. C., sailing from the Canal Zone on the *S.S. Santa Ines*.

May 31—The *Eleanor Bolling* with the bark *City of New York* in tow arrived at Balboa, Panama Canal Zone. The bark sailed from Dunedin, N. Z., on March 23.

June 3—Admiral Byrd with ships and crew sail for New York City.

June 19—The Admiral and his officers and men due to arrive in New York City, where they will receive the greeting of the populace.